HAUNTED
WIGAN

HAUNTED WIGAN

SARAH CARBERRY & NICOLA JOHNSON

The
History
Press

We would like to dedicate this book to the memory of Paul Reid, who
was an inspiration to us and to everyone in the paranormal world:
'Teams can work together and even support each other and we are proving that.'
Paul Reid 05.04.68 – 11.05.12
Rest in Peace, you will always be with us.

x

First published 2012
Reprinted 2012

The History Press
The Mill, Brimscombe Port
Stroud, Gloucestershire, GL5 2QG
www.thehistorypress.co.uk

© Sarah Carberry & Nicola Johnson, 2012

The right of Sarah Carberry & Nicola Johnson to be identified as the
Authors of this work has been asserted in accordance with the
Copyrights, Designs and Patents Act 1988.

British Library Cataloguing in Publication Data.
A catalogue record for this book is available from the British Library.

ISBN 978 0 7524 7481 6

Typesetting and origination by The History Press
Printed and bound in Great Britain by
Marston Book Services Limited, Didcot

Contents

Acknowledgements

WE would like to thank our friends and family, near and far. Also to Wigan Paranormal, a non-profit paranormal events and research team who provide support to Derian House Children's Hospice, and who have supported us every step of the way. We would like to thank the following people for their input into the publication: Stephen Speakman, Alex Parkinson, Cath O'Sullivan, Andrew Anson, Chris Patfield, Paul Cunliffe, Les Gaskill, Chris Bracek, Mrs M. Andrews, Estelle Hall and Dayna Hodgson. Also, a thank you to Gary Clee, who has provided the wonderful photographs for the book and the cover.

We would also like to thank our families for putting up with our unkempt homes and the lack of tea on the table; the members of public who stopped to speak to us and listen to our unusual requests; NatWest bank; Goldsmiths, and all of the other local shops which helped with our quest for information. Thanks to the pub landlords who allowed us to bend their ears over the bar. A thank you to Starbucks who provided us with all our caffeine and cake needs which, at times, was our core motivation.

Introduction

'An idea, like a ghost, must be spoken to a little before it will explain itself'

Charles Dickens

When you think of Wigan, what springs to mind? Maybe rugby or football? Maybe the famous Wigan Pier or Uncle Joe's Mint balls? Whatever it is, I am sure it won't be the ghosts that haunt the town, but as you read the real-life stories in this book you will discover there are plenty of memorable spooky tales and scary stories that will ensure you never look at Wigan in the same way again: from the bustling town centres where the spirits walk among the unsuspecting shoppers, to the towering abandoned mills with their dark corners, where ghostly children play hide and seek.

Wigan came into its own during the Industrial Revolution and was known as a major cotton mill and coal mining area. Coal mining started in 1450 and no fewer than 1,000 pit shafts were created around the town centre. In the 1800s, the cotton mills sprung into life employing men, women and children as young as nine. Sadly, working and living conditions left a lot to be desired and George Orwell wrote a book entitled *The Road to Wigan Pier*, in the hope of raising awareness of the dire situation. Many of the buildings from past years remain here to this day, re-fronted as a new property, but you only have to undertake some research to see that each building has its own tale and behind that, its own ghosts.

It is hard to imagine now, with the plush office suites and state-of-the-art shopping centres, that Wigan had such a bleak and dangerous past. Child mortality rates were high and a serious number of lives were lost in the mills and coal mines. If you were to take time out from the daily grind of Wigan life and wander around the mills, you would start to get a feeling of how vast industry was in the region. Child labour was a key part to the Industrial Revolution and Wigan didn't escape this. Many died at the hands of the large machines, and as a result of poor health and safety regulations. It was a way of life though, a far cry from the Wigan that we know and love in this modern day.

This book will look at the types of ghosts Wigan holds and also the different types of hauntings that take place under our very noses. Eyewitness accounts, old news stories and local legend make up the core ghost stories of Wigan. It seems that as soon as you mention the word 'ghost' in this area, everyone has a story and they are not afraid to share it. Ghosts seem to be a common way of life in Wigan and on a number of occasions have been happy to make themselves known. From local people living in fear from ghosts in their homes, to ghosts of highwaymen – there seem to be many stories and many sightings. Then there are the downright terrifying stories of cannibals and satanic worship, testing your palate for fear. Maybe you know someone who has told you these stories before and maybe you doubted them, but after listening to so many accounts, it is clearly obvious that Wigan ghosts are very much real. You can make your own mind up though; is it possible for so many people to see and hear the same things?

People often ask if George Formby has left a ghost behind, or maybe Fred Dibnah, but it seems their lives may have been all too happy to have felt the need to haunt the local area. Our Wigan ghosts seem a little more upset that they have passed away and are not afraid to show it.

So, take your seats on the number 666 bus as we take a tour around our historical town; remain seated because you never know where or when the next ghost might crop up. Let's visit the battlefields and the scenes of industrial tragedy, and pop into one of the many pubs for a spirit or two along the way. Keep your fingers inside though; some of our ghosts have been known to bite!

Sarah Carberry & Nicola Johnson, 2012

one

Types of Hauntings

Elementals

These are believed to be types of spirits or beings which inhabit nature, and are thought to possess supernatural powers. The belief of their existence was universal in the ancient era of religions and today many people still believe that all things possess life, especially occultists and neo-pagan witches.

Elementals are believed to exist as the life force in all living things; even the elements of earth, air, fire and water, the stars, zodiacs and the planets, are ruled by higher spirits called divas or archangels, and are generally thought to be benevolent creatures that maintain a natural harmony.

Some people describe them as evil or just mischievous, others say they are between angel and man and are able to materialize in animal or human form. They lack souls and seek sex with humans in order to acquire one, and are also capable of bearing children.

Some are said to be deceitful and hateful, causing tragic accidents and creating grief. They are associated with ritual magic and when sent on psychic attacks they attach themselves to human auras. If they are not dispelled when their mission is done, they can drain the energy from their victims and become confused and troublesome.

Poltergeists

There is slight controversy with regards to what a poltergeist actually is. 'Poltergeist' is a German word which means noisy spirit. What can you class as a noisy spirit? One that makes tapping noises, calls out a name, or one that throws objects? Some spirits can do one or all of these things, depending on how strong that energy is. Some believe that a poltergeist isn't a spirit at all, but psychokinetic energy which is caused by the subconscious mind of an individual. This person is often under physical, emotional or psychological stress and is often associated with young adults going through puberty. It is reported that poltergeists can turn lights on and off and effect other electrical appliances and make objects move; the manifestation of physical phenomena.

Intelligent Haunting

Residual Haunting

This is what most would call a classic haunting, where the spiritual entity is fully aware of the living world and if strong enough and willing to, will interact and respond to the living. In most cases this is because the spirit wishes to get the attention of the person, as it may be a relative or family friend. They will do this by moving objects, opening and closing doors, making parts of a room cold, giving you goosebumps, making sounds – like calling out your name – and even turning on lights, taps, TVs and radios. Sometimes they may be a bit more mischievous by throwing things or pushing people, this may be the result of the spirit not wanting you to be there, as you may be in what was once their home.

Normally, the prime time a spirit will show itself is between the hours of 11 p.m. and 3 a.m. This is because it takes a lot of energy for them appear (think of a flashlight shining during the day, you will hardly notice it, but turn the lights out...) although, very strong spirits have been known to be seen in daylight.

Some spirits are just lost souls that don't know what to do or are too scared to pass over; some don't even know they have died and carry on their day-to-day business.

There are many spirits who come back to their loved ones, to look over them and guide them through troubled times. There have been many times on investigations when we have encountered our own families with us, who are curious to know where we are going and wish to communicate with us.

These are the most commonly reported type of phenomena and also widely discounted by non-believers and scientists. The idea that actions are imprinted into an object or the environment can be very hard to comprehend and it can sometimes be difficult to understand, let alone explain, however, we will give it our utmost effort. I can, without doubt, confirm that it does exist; how and why is another matter as at times it does seem to defy the laws of energy and physics, but that is the beauty of the paranormal – it does not need to have any real scientific basis to support it.

Residual hauntings are not what we call an actual haunting, as there is no inhuman or human interaction at all, but it does display past events. These types of hauntings are like a reel of film playing in a loop over and over again. As to why it happens and what is it, no official explanation exists, but with research and many years of study the paranormal world has a pretty accurate conclusion.

These audible or visual 'films' are past events which are imprinted into the environment by a certain type of energy, this is called the Stone Tape Theory; a paranormal hypothesis that was brought about in the 1970s as a possible explanation for ghosts. These events usually occur in the same spot, whether the past event was a suicide, accidental death, murder or torture, and sometimes in happy times, you may hear music from another era. Certain materials, such as crystals, water, limestone and sandstone have excellent qualities for absorbing energy from living beings and you may find a lot of supernatural activity around where they are.

two

Public Houses

MOST people you speak to in Wigan about hauntings will point you in the direction of a public house. These historic watering holes have been used for many, many years, not only as a place of rest for the living but at times as a morgue or a hideout. Tunnels make their way underneath the streets of Wigan, spilling out into public houses and bringing, sometimes, a little more then a draught.

The Mount

Probably the most famous haunted pub in Wigan is The Mount. Many people have spent a cold, dark night in this beautiful building and its cellars in the hope of catching a glimpse of just one of its ghosts. The Mount has an interesting history and can be traced back to the Domesday Book. This once magnificent home of Abraham Guest and his family is now a well-established restaurant, which is busy both day and night.

As you enter through the front door, you are met by a grand staircase with a wide balcony. Standing at the balcony edge, the apparition of a young girl has been seen watching and smiling. She is thought to have fallen over the edge to her death. Many customers and staff have seen the little girl. One member of staff reported her own daughter playing with a little girl at the top of the stairs and when her mother was taken to greet the mystery girl, it became apparent the girl was, in fact, a ghost. Another story associated with the girl on the stairs is that she was actually killed outside, in front of the building, when it was once a family home. She is thought to play on the stairs and run around the rooms as if she was still alive. An eyewitness describes what he saw:

> In the early 1970s, my wife and I worked as assistant managers at The Mount, which was, at the time, a Chef & Brewer restaurant. One morning we both arrived at work and up the stairs walked a girl in a summer dress. She passed us and went

into what was then the ladies' toilet on the ground floor. It was a February morning and it was raining heavily. Only the cleaning staff were in and I checked if any had brought a child to work. None had and it became quite a talking point. My wife was convinced we'd seen a ghost. A few weeks later, two nuns came in and asked to speak to us about what we had seen. They told us a little girl had lived in the house and was knocked down by a tram in front of the house – the ladies' toilet the little girl had walked into had once been the child's playroom.

Venturing up a winding staircase onto the third floor, a feeling of hopelessness and fear surrounds you. At the top of this staircase there is the reported sad ghost of a man who hung himself and who now walks the stairs full of regret.

Many women have said they have felt heavily pregnant and heard sobbing whilst being in one room in particular. The spirit of a young pregnant woman is said to haunt this room after being beaten and left for dead.

The cellars are a warren of tunnels, each as eerie as the next. One of the rooms was used to store bodies of the local people prior to burial, and the ghost of what can only be described as an undertaker lurks in the shadows. It is said that the room could sometimes be full of bodies and the small bearded man showed no respect as he climbed over them, breaking bones where he lay his feet. The cracking of bones can still be heard to this day echoing around the cellar. He is seen wheeling a cart through the cellars, moving the bodies to their resting places.

As you walk down the dark, cold tunnel you come across another room which is closed off by a door. Opening the door you see a staircase that leads to a locked door and it is clear that the passage behind it is no longer in use. This used to be the servant's entrance and in this small space a dark and chilling secret is held. The ghost of a young woman has been seen at the bottom of the staircase and she can be heard sobbing. The woman was found murdered at the bottom of the steps and still haunts the area to this day.

Back through the tunnels, a nun, Sister Magdalene, wanders, looking for the children hiding down there, afraid of their punishment. One visitor claimed that she spoke to a girl crouched in the corner, who said she had been abused. As she put her hand out to touch the girl she disappeared, and her quiet sobs a second or two after.

It is also believed that the spirit of the architect haunts one room in particular, the Rivington Room. Plans of the building are still to this day displayed on the wall and it is possible that he visits the site of his work as a form of pride, or to keep an eye on it.

A few years ago, a member of staff had some money go missing from his pocket. It was taken as a serious matter and eventually the police were involved, but the matter was never resolved. One night, a medium went into the pub; he knew nothing of this event or even the history behind the building, but he was asked to pass on a message to the pub manager. The ghost of a young man wanted to say he was sorry and that he didn't mean to cause so much trouble. When the medium asked what he had done, the spirit replied he had taken some paper from a pocket and it has the number twenty on each sheet. He only did it as a joke and it ended with everyone being so angry. So, the mystery was resolved but it was never confirmed who the ghost of the young man was. However, although the ghost has moved items and played tricks on people since then, he has never touched money again.

In 2008, The Mount and its ghost stories was in the news and an article was published about the ongoing sightings. The story went on to talk about Agnes and Joe Fox from Glasgow, who, visiting friends in Wigan, found themselves in The Mount's hotel – the Orrell Premier Inn. Agnes was woken from her sleep late at night by a man standing over her bed. As Agnes screamed with fear the ghostly figure disappeared. After researching the hotel on the internet she realised that what she had witnessed was not an unusual occurrence, although she had never mentioned it whilst there, for fear of being ridiculed. Agnes stated:

We were in room number six and it was in the middle of the night when I woke up suddenly to see this man just standing there looking at me. He was white, 30 to 35-years-old with a squarish face and well-kept mousy to brown hair. He was wearing a suit which would be in fashion in the 1950s or 60s. I was quite startled but not exactly frightened. One moment he was there, the next he wasn't. If he was a ghost, then the dead can't harm you anyway. That experience won't stop us coming back to the Premier Inn at Orrell because the service, facilities and the staff were wonderful. We might not have the same room though.

The Mount Hotel, where spirits lurk beyond the bar.

Upon asking The Mount for a response to the claims, the duty manager Rob Hale said:

> It could well be true. There have been quite a few sightings at both The Mount and Premier Inn. The latter is built on an old nunnery and its graves, and all sorts of figures have been seen. I once saw a lady and a cat one night at The Mount upstairs. She was wearing old Victorian clothing. The cat went into the function rooms but then disappeared. I couldn't find it and there was no other way out.

Rob also goes on to say, 'The reputation for ghosts doesn't seem to be putting people off. No one comes to any harm and people are intrigued by it. In fact, we have had ghost walks and séances.'

So, if you are ever visiting Wigan and want a truly haunted experience, book in for a stay at The Mount and say hello to its many ghosts.

Legs of Man Hotel

The arcade once stood here, and it was an old favourite for all Wiganers, but was unfortunately demolished to make way for the Marketgate shopping arcade. It was here where you could buy your pots and pans, washing tubs, scrubbing boards, or get weighed on Bob's weighing chair, and the famous Gorners Café used to tempt you with the aroma of hot food – the specialty being hotpot with red cabbage. There was a pub here called the Legs of Man Hotel, which is an incredibly long pub – it was so long it had two nicknames; 'top legs' and 'bottom legs'. It was supposed to be haunted by the ghost of Lord Derby, when it was called the Old Dogg Inn; he was nursed here after being wounded in the Civil War. It is stipulated that it is in the arcade where 'Big Norm' roams. Norman Melling, from Pemberton, fought Bill D'arcy over a mutual sweetheart, Mary Hogan. Norman died from his injuries and is believed to be searching for D'arcy to reap revenge before he can be reunited with his loved one

The Stork Inn

Anyone who has travelled through Billinge will have seen this beautiful black and white building standing on the corner, welcoming people into the town. Inside, the main feature is a staircase taken from a sixteenth-

The Legs of Man Hotel – now demolished to make way for the Marketgate shopping arcade.

century manor house, and even this stairway features its own ghost; the ghost of a girl who fell down them and died from her injuries.

This magnificent pub holds some secrets, especially within the tunnels, which are said to lead from its cellars to St Aiden's Church and the Crank Caves. Built in 1640, the building once stood as a toll tower and also served as a darker purpose: a jail. Within the cellars there used to be a torture bed with shackles, which are still attached to the wall. It is said that a cavalier was tortured to death here and that his ghost still haunts the building to this day; he is known to sit by the fire.

The ghost of an intoxicated man has been seen in the men's toilets and is heard making noises at night; this is possibly a local ghost who visits the place, just as he did while he was alive.

The ghost of local 1920s highwayman, George Lyon, who was often seen drinking in this hotel, still frequents this public house, as well as galloping on his horse through the village.

There is a previous landlord, by the name of George, who keeps a watchful eye on the pub and the new landlords. He has been seen behind the bar and is quite often mistaken for bar staff by unsuspecting public.

A hooded figure has been seen hanging from a beam in the cellar. It is unkown if he was murdered or committed suicide, but his ghost still lingers, trapped in the moment of his own death.

During the 1960s, a barmaid came running from the cellar in terror. She refused to go back down there again. Minutes later, all the glasses on the bar started to shake and although the staff tried to find a reason for this, they were unable to. Could this have been connected to the man hanging in the cellar, angry that his life was snatched from him or in regret for taking his own life?

The Stork Inn in Billinge, Wigan.

The Honeysuckle Pub

In 2008, the Honeysuckle pub in Poolstock appeared in the local paper due to spooky goings-on. The landlord, John Purnell, who was running the establishment at the time, reported that both he and his family had had strange experiences, as well as the regulars. The sightings consisted of a young lady dressed in what seemed to be a 1960s-style raincoat. She walked through the bar then disappeared! This ghost is sometimes seen with a younger girl, and there was a suggestion that the girl's name was Lucy, who was just six years old when she perished due to smoke damage, and that the lady is her mother, looking throughout the pub to find her. One local had a deep conversation with these ghosts before they disappeared before his very eyes. The landlord's daughter saw a second reflection standing next to her in the mirror and his granddaughter has felt someone blowing in her face and has heard whispering.

Although these ghost stories seem unsettling, it is the cellar that holds the most frightening tales; prisoners held captive 400 years ago, awaiting their departure to Preston along the river, and one lingering spirit called Harris, who is said to be dressed in a black coat buttoned up high. The door to the cellar once locked itself from the inside, the key mysteriously breaking off and leaving the entrance sealed until the door was forced open.

Berkeley Square

The Berkley Square, which was once the Minorca Hotel, was listed in the *Haunted Pub Guide* (1985) and reported in *Lancashire's Ghosts and Legends*, written by Terence W. Whittaker. There is a tale that tells of pint pots which would fill after all the pumps had been switched off. Landlords, Jon and Vicky Ambrose, spoke to the local paper about their encounters, stating that their dog refused to go into certain areas, furniture was moved about and cold spots were felt.

Cherry Gardens

The legend of the Cherry Gardens on Wigan Road says that the body of a baby was hidden in a fireplace and that his distraught parents still haunt the area today. The landlords of the pub, afraid of previous activity, invited a medium along to find out who was haunting the building. Following that, a team of paranormal investigators held an overnight vigil and found that, along with the distressed parents, there were a number of spirits in the pub; amongst them a man who had worked in the coaching house, who loved the Cherry Gardens so much he has continued to reside there after death. Also, the sprit of a lady has been seen and heard in the living quarters looking for her son, who was thought to have died in the bathroom.

As with many of the other Wigan public houses and inns, there is said to be a tunnel travelling from the pub to various locations, including Haigh Hall and the local church. These particular tunnels are said to be home to a number of ghostly monks looking for the way out after hiding away throughout the Dissolution of the Monastries, during Henry VIII's reign.

The Fleece

The Fleece Hotel in Ashton-in-Makerfield is reportedly home to over 200 ghosts. The landlady herself has seen many ghostly figures and has even managed to capture them on film. She reported seeing shadows and hearing footsteps all around her, and was shocked at what she saw on her night vision security cameras. Seemingly out of nowhere, there were people walking past the camera, but the pub was shut and in darkness: she was alone. Face after face appeared on the camera, hour after hour, until it finally trailed off and the camera showed an empty pub again. Paranormal investigators visited The Fleece Hotel, in order to get to the bottom of the hauntings, and were able to help some of the people pass over, leaving maybe ten lost souls still pacing the pub.

The building has now been split into more business but strange goings-on are still known to happen in the now separate areas of the premises, namely in a beauty salon and a hairdressers. History has it that a man was found murdered in the cellar of the hairdressers and his ghost still lurks there today, seen and felt by members of staff. One witness recalls that she was in the cellar, mixing a colour for a customer, when she saw a man standing in the corner. Knowing that no one else should be down there, she turned to call down another member of staff, but when she looked back towards the corner the man was nowhere to be seen.

The Old Pear Tree

The very old, yet pretty building which The Old Pear Tree occupies has been rumoured to host a poltergeist for a number of years. The landlady, Lynn Watson, spoke to the local paper in 2003 about the strange goings-on and even stated that she had named the ghost George. She had witnessed items going missing, crisp packets being thrown across the bar, the TV turning itself up, something touching and tugging on her legs and light bulbs exploding. But Lynn's seventeen-year-old daughter, Katie, had a completely different kind of encounter with George: face-to-face. Katie recalled that, 'He was in his seventies and wears an old wax full-length jacket. He's very dishevelled looking. One time he threw a glass at the cleaner. It smashed on the floor and I could clearly hear it crunching under an invisible foot.' George has even been caught on camera in the form of floating lights, which moved towards a door which is no longer there.

In 2011, a team of ghost-hunters stayed in the pub over night to see if they could record any of this paranormal activity. What they caught on film and audio that night can not be explained. Everyone was sitting in the bar area when what sounded like heavy footsteps suddenly stamped across the ceiling, culminating with an almighty bang that shook the walls. After many attempts to re-enact the noise they found it was impossible and whatever was making itself known was clearly a strong and determined spirit.

The Pagefield Hotel

Standing tall and proud, The Pagefield Hotel, or The Famous Pagefield as it is now known, is a magnificent building steeped in history. The pub itself has stood on this spot since 1902 and this date can be seen written in the beautiful stained-glass windows. There have been many ghost stories attached to this building. The most famous is that of a little girl who has been spotted running up the grand staircase and watching people drink from the top, behind the banisters

The spirits of a man and a woman are also thought to haunt the pub and it has been suggested that they are the young girl's parents. Her mother, according to legend, committed suicide, unable to cope with her grief after losing her daughter. Her ghost has been seen standing by an upstairs window and sometimes on the ledge, as if ready to jump.

A soldier has also been seen, standing in the corner of one of the bedrooms. He has been heard calling out for his sister who, as the tale goes, he returned from war to see. It is thought that his spirit will not rest until he is reunited with his sister.

The third floor of this building has been untouched for 100 years and is an ideal playground for the many ghosts who remain in this beautiful building. A photograph taken in one of the bedrooms quite clearly shows the face of a little girl. She was named Molly by a medium, but it is not known if this is the same little girl who runs up and down the stairs in the bar area.

A paranormal investigation taking place in The Pagefield Hotel.

The Boars Head

The Boars Head, on the way into Standish, is one of the oldest public houses in the country, dating back to 1271, and is also featured in the Domesday Book. Used in the fifteenth century as a last stop-off for prisoners on their way to be hung in Lancaster, it holds a grisly tale. The condemned were held in the cellar awaiting their fate; one such prisoner has remained there in spirit and still haunts the Boars Head cellar.

A second ghost has been encountered in the billiards room – a man wearing a top hat who speaks with an upper-class accent. There is also a rumour that a previous landlord hanged himself in the pub and he may now haunt the pub too.

The Old Springs

The Old Springs in Kitt Green was once a family farmhouse which has now become a homely public house. Its cellars were once used as a morgue for the surrounding village, where bodies were kept until they could be buried. There are many ghost stories surrounding the pub and a dark figure has been seen in the cellar. A local customer named Diane told of her visit to the cellar:

I was told of the ghost in the cellar but I wanted to witness it for myself. Not thinking I would catch anything, I nonetheless took a video camera down and waited. After a while I went to shut off my camera. As I did I saw a number of bright white lights across the night vision screen and the battery just drained. I reached for my torch but as I flicked this on, the battery also drained. I was left in the pitch black. After a few minutes my eyes adjusted and I could make out the barrels and the doorway. Suddenly, the room went very dark. I could no longer see the door but I could see the barrels, it was as if something was blocking the door. I decided to leave and come back with a working torch but as I made my way to where I thought the doorway and stairs were, I felt a cold breath on my face and the right-hand side of my body went freezing cold. I could now see the door though and I carried on towards it. As I got there, a pitch-black figure stepped in front of it. I thought the room was dark as it was but this figure was black and solid. I asked who it was but there was no sound, it just stood there. I reached out my hand and the figure remained, although where my hand touched it was like touching icy air. Feeling in danger I decided I had to leave and I rushed towards the door and up the stairs. I felt myself break through an icy wall of air and as I came back up into the pub I felt sick and dizzy. After my account other people went down and some said they saw a dark figure too.

The strangest story connected to The Old Springs is that of a photograph of the old house, which is still on show inside the pub today. The photograph depicts a family gathering, but away to the side there is a little girl, who appears to be clutching a doll. The girl did not belong to the family, nor is there any recollection of her being there at the time the photograph was taken (*c.* 1900s). It has remained a mystery ever since. Next time you are passingby, pop in and ask to see the photo, the landlord will gladly point you to the right wall.

The Bellingham Hotel

Once a row of houses, this now large hotel – situated directly across from the hospital – is home to a number of ghosts. Members of staff have reported seeing a man in the kitchen and he has even spoken to them, saying good morning and asking for the time.

More eerily, in the attic space, which remains as it was, there is a ghost of a deformed man who was kept up there when alive, to be hidden away from the public eye. He peers through the open beams and hides in the shadows, as if locked in a timeless misery.

In the cellars, which were once the ground floor of the houses, there is said to be the ghost of a priest, who is thought to have been trapped down in the tunnels that lead to Haigh Hall. A small boy also cowers in the corner, afraid of a man who is covered in dirt. Staff that have ventured into the cellars have been touched, pushed and felt breath on their faces, only to realise that they were alone.

The Bellingham Hotel, Wigan.

The Bowling Green

The owner and staff at The Bowling Green have witnessed the spooky figure of a lady wrapped in a blue shawl walking through the bar. Bar stools mysteriously move by themselves, and the apparition of a man sitting at the end of the bar waits to be served, who, when the bar staff turn to serve him, disappears into thin air.

The John Bull Chophouse

One of the oldest pubs in Wigan, The John Bull Chophouse, stands on The Wiend, the oldest street in Wigan. Once split into three cottages it was home to three families, one of which still resides there in spirit. The ghost of a middle-aged woman makes herself known to staff and customers and is still proud of her small home to this day. At the far right-hand side of the pub, is the ghost of a confused man, who feels he is misunderstood. He can seem quite angry and negative, but that is simply his way.

Upstairs, in the pool room, the ghost of a young man has been seen pacing the floor. Legend has it that he took his own life – he hanged himself from the beams – and has been trapped in that room ever since. Sometimes, in the dead of night when everything else is still, you can hear the spine-tingling sound of a swinging rope rubbing against the wood.

The middle cottage was transformed into an oyster bar and the small thriving business is the haunt ghost of a jolly man who

The John Bull Chophouse, one of the oldest pubs in Wigan.

once wheeled his cart through the town. He has been seen, smartly dressed, outside the pub with his cart.

Back at the bar there are a couple of ghostly punters who sit and wait for their drink. One man, who used to drink there regularly, was a biker who was killed suddenly in a tragic accident. He is angry that his life was taken away and comes back to his favourite pub for a drink. So, next time you're sat at the bar of the John Bull, just turn to the side and say hello.

The Wheatsheaf Pub, Westhoughton

The landlord of this pub reported that his dog would be interested in one room and react as if something was there which the landlord couldn't see himself. Many people claim to have seen a ghost in the pub, which would disappear but leave a shadow that would remain for a good few seconds.

Ex-Serviceman's Club, Westhoughton

The Lady in Red is said to haunt this ex-serviceman's club. No one knows who she is or her reason for haunting the club, but she leaves a rose-tinted mist as she travels around the room and has been seen on a number of occasions.

The Boulevard

This underground pub with no windows already holds a certain atmosphere, but it is thought that it was once used for satanic worship and bloodletting. A dark-cloaked man has been seen circling the room; maybe looking for the next sacrifice. One witness claimed that she could even feel a swish of air as he passed her by.

In 2007, the Boulevard made the local news when a medium visited in an attempt to explain the paranormal activity plaguing the bar. Children's voices were heard and then recorded, and ghostly shadows were seen in the mirrors by most of the staff. It was discovered that the function room was used to store bodies before they went for burial. The medium confirmed that:

> There's a man who is very angry. He was quite solitary and spent a lot of time alone, so of course, being confined to a pub, he is not happy. He's a macabre and sinister figure, and wears a white apron. He's definitely trapped in this life or in this plane and not gone over to the spirit world. In his mind he is protecting the bodies.

Gallimores Bar and Resturaunt

Situated on The Wiend, this first-class restaurant is home to a ghost. If you ask any of the staff who Albert is, they will tell you that he is their ghost and that he has been seen many times. He was sadly crushed to death under a cart and his spirit has remained in the same spot ever since. The cellars are connected to tunnels that lead to the parish church and they run not only under the Gallimores Bar and Restaurant, but a selection of other public houses in the town.

The White Lion, Upholland

This public house is believed by many to be one of the most haunted in the North West. The landlord has encountered many ghosts, and reports of sightings have been given by customers and staff; pool balls moving on their own; ghostly children heard running around; voices, groans and footsteps; cold spots felt and the sensation of being touched. This pub also sits directly across from the grave of George Lyon, who was the last highwayman to be hanged at Lancaster Castle. His ghost is said to haunt The White Lion to this day, returning to finish his last pint.

The landlord of The While Lion has hosted charity ghost nights and everyone involved experienced something spooky, proving that this public house has customers from both this life and the next.

The Orwell

This pub is situated on Wigan Pier and is comprised of two parts; the pub itself and the museum building, 'The Way We Were', which is now disused.

Many paranormal investigations have been carried out in this building and one group, Shadow Seekers, have been into the property twice, following reports of hauntings by staff, who have felt the presence of a man who stands and watches what is transpiring. They have named this ghost 'George' as he was felt in the George Orwell Suite. As well as doors opening and

The Orwell, named after George Orwell, author of The Road to Wigan Pier.

Gallimore's Fine Restaurant, where the resident ghost is part of the fixtures and fittings.

closing on their own, other paranormal activity reported include a negative atmosphere, being touched, and the temperature dropping suddenly.

Another spirit which haunts this public house is that of the chef, who died of a heart attack a few years ago. His ghost has been felt in the kitchen and dining area, as if to check that his work is being carried on to a high standard.

Eckersley Mills

As you head out of the town centre, towering above the famous Wigan Pier are the old cotton mills. These grand buildings were once a part of a massive industrial site but are now, sadly, mostly derelict. The odd business occupies some of the spaces in the mills and the employees have plenty of stories to tell about the spirits left behind.

Originally, the mills were broken down into sections and even had their own hospital and chiropodist to ensure that their workers were looked after. Pregnant women would be taken from their workstation straight into the infirmary to give birth, enabling them to work for as long as possible. Although some have happy memories of the mills, others have distressing memories, resulting from the lack of health and safety regulations at that time; most positions in the mills held a risk factor and sadly, the loss of life during the milling years was vast.

Even today, you only have to walk around the buildings to feel uneasy. They look and feel haunted and as soon as you speak to people who have worked there, you realise that they actually *are* haunted.

As you drive into the vicinity, the words 'DEAD SLOW' send out a clear message that this was a busy site. The architecture, however, is stunningly beautiful and the entrances appear grand. It is not hard to imagine how this all looked in its prime. The date 1908 is crafted into the brickwork and there seems to be endless windows looking out across Wigan.

Before the mills finally closed, workers had already recorded witnessing strange happenings; reels of cotton flying across the rooms, the feeling of being touched, cold spots and weird shadows. One lady can clearly recall the eery feelings she experienced on an almost daily basis.

'Dead Slow' entrance to Eckersley Mills.

She described what happened the first time she witnessed paranormal activity at work:

> I was setting up work for the day and I had placed a reel of cotton next to me that I was about to load. The reel was large and quite heavy but in front of my eyes I saw it tip up on its side then roll across the table and on to the floor. I picked it back up and put it down, but as soon as I had set it down, the reel was on the floor again. I put it back on my workstation and walked away, feeling slightly scared. I spoke to a friend and we both turned to look at the reel in question, and, as if on demand, the reel rolled off the table again. An older colleague came over and laughed, telling me I was being played with. I must have looked frightened because she put her arm round me and just said I will get used to them. Them? I questioned who she meant and she told me it was the ghosts of children and that sometimes they just want to play. It was an everyday occurrence. Since that day, I was afraid to work there and I did see and hear things I just couldn't explain. Everyone there knew it was a ghost and just carried on their work around them.

Since the mills have been closed a lot of paranormal activity has been highlighted by current occupiers and security staff. A number of mediums and paranormal teams have attended the area, coming up with the same information each time and never disappointed with the evidence of hauntings. Numerous photographs showing bright

Orbs captured at Eckersley Mills.

More orbs captured at night around Eckersley Mills.

Industrial machinery was responsible for the loss of many lives in the mills.

Cotton looms like these were used at Eckersley Mills. Such machinery was the cause of tragic accidents and sometimes death.

lights and mists have been produced and to this day the ghost-hunting still goes on.

At the rear of the mills, where the goods were dispatched, a terrible accident occurred and one man was crushed to death in the 1950s. He still haunts the spot and his footsteps can be heard, loud and clear, as he continues to carry out his job. Witnesses have said that he sometimes stops to stare and can be seen standing in doorways observing everything that is going on, before heading back to complete his job. This apparition is not alone, as in the same mill a small boy has been seen running down the corridors and peering out of windows towards the people below. Children were a common site in cotton mills as they were small enough

to squeeze behind the machines should something go wrong. However, this was a dangerous job and could result in a loss of limb, which was life-threatening, especially for small children who could bleed to death very quickly. The ghosts of children have been seen throughout all of the mill buildings and giggles have been heard, as if they are hiding in the shadows.

Even the old dining hall has its share of ghosts. Whilst the mills were in operation, the dining hall was used to feed all of the workers, but even these parts of the mills saw tragic deaths.

Whilst working on the restoration of the mills, one workman reported seeing the ghost of a man running across the room then suddenly stopping and dropping to the floor. It was later discovered that a man had died here after suffering a heart attack; he had tried to get help but collapsed before he could reach the door. Following this incident, many other people have witnessed the ghost of the panicking man.

Around the same area, a woman has been seen clutching her throat and choking sounds have been heard echoing around the building. The records do show that a woman choked in the dining room whilst eating her lunch and died. Her spirit seems to appear between the hours of twelve and two and it has been reported that a lot of activity happens between these times, reflecting the time in which the hall was most in use. The clattering of dishes can be heard and some-

Eckersley Mills, where the face of a small child has been seen at the window.

Trencherfield Mills and the canal.

times the smell of cooking fills the air, as if it was 1915 and lunch time was in full swing.

Other reports from the dining hall include the sound of a heavy sack being dragged across the floor, which can sometimes go on for minutes; voices calling out; whistling; flashing lights; temperature changes and people being physically touched. Some people have claimed to have seen a man walking towards them, arms swinging, only to realise that he his standing in one place. Feelings of pregnancy and childbirth have also been reported and it is thought a woman died during childbirth in the building, leaving her tortured spirit behind for other people to encounter.

Looking up at the vast windows, shadows and faces have been seen passing by. The buildings themselves are now empty and secured, but security staff have reported seeing people in the buildings, only to find, upon further investigation, that they are empty of physical beings. Alarms are tripped regularly, which has, quite often, happened in the same zones where ghostly sightings have been witnessed, with no plausible reason. Businesses in the older mills have reported strange sensations and witnessed their stock moving around with no apparent explanation.

Some of the oldest areas of the mills date back to the 1800s. Connecting Wigan to the rest of the country with the canal and Wigan Pier, Eckersley Mills was, and still is, a very important part of Wigan's heritage. It is no wonder that these amazing buildings have left behind so many memories, along with the spirits of those who helped to create them.

Eckersley Mills, a reminder of industrial Wigan.

Bygone Times

The Grove Mill stands in an area known as 'The Green'. It was once used as a temporary army encampment by the Parliamentarians after the siege of Lathom during the English Civil War. Colonel Alexander Rigby was in command, but they were later defeated by Royalist forces at Bolton.

Grove Mill was used in the seventeenth century for woollen processing; Brookes Mill came into production in the eighteenth century as a corn mill and Millbrook house, with the cobbled alleyway which you pass on your way to Bygone Times, dates back even earlier. This is now used as

Ariel view of Bygone Times.

the building's main offices, with four members of staff. Thirty ghosts that have been accounted for up to now.

Bygone Times, an old mill which is today an antiques and collectors' centre.

Syd Brook Grove Works was built in the 1830s as a calico printing works; this was powered by two large waterwheels on the works lodge and was owned by Thomas Bentley. After his death in 1844, the business was sold on to become part of a large complex of mills when Grove Mill was built in 1845.

By 1861 the mill was employing 300 people in spinning and weaving production, under the ownership of John Jacob Smalley (trading as John Smalley, Sykes & Co.). A fire seriously destroyed the spinning machinery and mill buildings in September 1875 and a lot of the families who worked at Grove Mill left the village after being laid off.

In 1884, Mr Ibzan Sagar and his business partner purchased Grove Mill for a sum of £1,150. Unfortunately, the business soon found itself in financial difficulty, having to honour contracts with the previous suppliers and paying above the market price for yarn. Luckily, Carrington & Woods came to the rescue and purchased the mill in 1895, appointing Ibzan Sagar as manager on a salary of £35 a week. This was the start of a great future for Grove Mill; it produced parachutes during the Second World War for the British Airborne Forces and became the largest rayon weaving mill in the world after a merger with Viyella in 1970.

In the early 1980s, Grove Mill ceased production and some older parts of the mill were demolished and other areas were let out as industrial units. By the late 1980s, John Rigby and the present owner Mr Tim Knowles began a redevelopment of the mill and turned it into Bygone Times, an antiques and collectors' centre.

When you visit Bygone Times, ask any member of staff and they will happily provide you with a ghost guide – as you browse the mill looking for wonderful items to spend your money on, you can try and see if you can find the ghosts, free of charge.

An apparition of a gentleman in a 1920s suit has been witnessed by more than one person, pacing up and down the main aisle on level 1. In the far end of Millbrook house three spirits have been witnessed; from a window facing the cobbled alleyway (which was the main thoroughfare through the site) the face of a lady has been seen – she is believed to be waiting for the imminent arrival of either a loved one or a family member; a spirit by the name of Florence can be heard as she sits in her rocking chair, the wooden floorboards creaking under the chair. It is believed that something quite disturbing is hidden in the fireplace in Millbrook House – no one has dared look yet, and the owners of Bygone Times have advised people not to!

On level 2, in the heater area, there is a spirit called Patrick Scott. He was an overseer in the weaving shed and has been seen hurriedly pacing the floor, rapping his stick against objects, obviously a little miffed about something.

In Lower Millbrook House, the apparitions of two cheeky children have been seen misbehaving outside the lower floor, which used to be a meeting room used for religious purposes.

In the aisle of level 3, outside the penny arcade, there have been sightings of two apparitions – a tall lady and a gentleman both dressed in Victorian clothing, strolling past the entrance hand-in-hand.

When the old penny arcade machines were moved into the building, Bygone Times seemed to acquire an extra visitor. A man called Arthur Jones, who used to be the arcade manager in the early Edwardian era, is a little attached to one machine and has stayed with it ever since.

On the ground floor of the whole building there have been sightings of ghostly outlines of small children running around; sometimes cries of pain have also been heard. It is well documented that small children, who worked in the weaving sheds at the time, were often badly injured and sometimes killed whilst they were climbing through the machinery.

On the riverbank, down the old cobbled alleyway, the spectral figure of a lady has been seen walking from Heskin to Syd Brook (Grove Mill) late at night.

three

Stately Homes

Ackhurst Hall

There have been sightings of a ghost girl in and around the property of Ackhurst Hall, in Gathurst. She is believed to be Annie Houghton, who lived with her family in a converted barn about 200 metres from the hall. The hall was owned by Mr Roper and Mr Houghton was his farm bailiff, who had been his confidential clerk for a number of years and was well-respected in the area.

It was a Tuesday evening when the tragedy happened. The date was 15 December 1868, and at around half past six Mr Houghton went to Gathurst Station to meet Mr Roper. Mrs Houghton had gone to the hall to milk the cows and left Annie, their eldest daughter, in charge of their other daughter Katie, who was nine years old. Annie was only twelve years old but she was entrusted to look after her sister as long as she kept the door locked while her parents were away. Mr Houghton returned with Mr Roper at around quarter to eight and as they crossed the lane they met a man called Parkinson, an under manager at one of Mr Roper's collieries on the estate, who accompanied them on the path to the hall door.

On her way back to the barn, Mrs Houghton saw a flock of ducks lying on the grass; well, that is what she thought it was until she reached the spot There, lying in the grass, in a pool of blood, was the body of little Annie. Her screams brought the others running to the scene and Mr Roper stayed with the body while the others rushed to the barn. The kitchen was empty. The mother began shouting out in agony for Katie and they heard her muffled cries in a nearby field. Katie, badly injured but conscious, told her parents that the door was locked until Annie opened it to get coal for the fire from the yard at about 7 p.m. She described how a man, taller than her father, had appeared at the door asking about her father and if he lived there. Annie explained that her father was at the hall, as she assumed that they would have been back from the station, but before she could show the man the direction in which to go, she was struck with a heavy hammer

Ackhurst Hall in Gathurst, Wigan.

on her forehead. This didn't knock her down and he chased poor Annie around the kitchen striking blows; blood splattered the walls as she fled. Annie escaped through the door and attempted to go around the barn to get to the hall, but she was caught and another blow from the hammer to her head sent her to the ground, where she was found. The man then returned to the barn and struck Katie with a blow to the back of her head and several to the shoulder. When she stayed on her feet he grabbed her around the throat and squeezed tightly and, thinking he had strangled her, threw her over the hedge and into the field.

Luckily, the two small boys upstairs and the baby in the crib in the kitchen were unharmed. It was thought to be a robbery as there was a silver watch missing, which had been in a cupboard in the ransacked kitchen. Also, it was well known that as a farm bailiff Mr Houghton had sums of money in the house to pay the farm labourers. They found the hammer near the back door; it was a hammer similar to the ones used in the collieries.

Although a reward was offered for the capture of the murderer, he was never found, and little Annie's lost soul is said to relive the nightmare of that fateful night.

Haigh Hall and Lady Mabel

The word 'Haigh' is taken from the Old English *Haga*, which means 'the enclosure', and it has been variously recorded as Hage in 1193, Hagh in 1298, and Haghe, Ha, and Haw in the sixteenth century.

Haigh Hall is an extensive estate that was rebuilt in 1800 using stone from the local quarry in Parbold, and later, in 1860, plantains were laid out after the disfigurement of the landscape caused from coal mining.

There have been many ghostly goings-on within the hall and, to this day, the top two floors of the hall are still as it was years ago,

Haigh Hall, where Lady Mabel haunts the grounds.

Lady Mabel.

now derelict and unsafe in places. In the 1970s, a ghost hunter ventured up to the very top floor and had a nervous breakdown after seeing a figure clad in a long, white, shroud-like garment and what seemed to be a black executioner's hood. Who could this be? One explanation is that it is James Stanley, the former Earl of Derby, who was wounded and captured after his part in the Battle of Wigan Lane in 1651. James Stanley was executed at Bolton, but on his way to his final resting place in Ormskirk he was kept overnight at Haigh Hall, with his head and body in separate boxes.

In the famous Mabs Gallery there have been numerous accounts of poltergeist activity, and a figure of a Grey Lady has been seen, but no one knows who she is.

A ghostly lady has been seen looking out of the first-floor window, which was formally a bedroom but is now the ladies' toilets…what, or who, is she looking for?

On the second floor, a male servant is said to roam; people often report being pushed or have felt a breath on the back of their necks.

The most famous story of Haigh Hall is that of Lady Mabel. Mabel le Norreys was born in 1274, and was the daughter of

Hugh le Norreys, Lord of Blackrod and the owner of Haigh. Following her father's death, Mabel (who was a minor) was placed in the guardianship of Richard Bradshaw and his family, who were, at that time, the occupiers of Haigh Hall.

In 1295, she married William Bradshaw, son of Richard Bradshaw. One tale says that Mabel was ignorant to the fact that she was the heir of Haigh, Blackrod and Westleigh, and William discovered this by some means and sought her out. He found Mabel cooking oatcakes in the kitchen and said, 'Maid, if thou wilt marry me, I will make thee lady of Haigh, Blackrod and Westleigh', and, of course, she agreed.

In 1315, William went to war and then fled the country after his part in the Banastre Rebellion. Mabel heard no news of William and after some time he was presumed dead. She married a Welsh knight, thought to be called Henry Teuther, but, as the story goes, Sir William returned home in 1324, dressed as a palmer (a pilgrim) and carried, as a disguise, a staff covered with a palm leaf. Across his shoulder was a large bag full of food that he had begged along the way. He wore a long cloak that reached his feet, which was also used as a blanket during the night. When Lady Mabel saw him, she was immediately reminded of her first husband, and wept uncontrollably. Her husband, Henry, asked her the reason for her tears and when she told him, he struck her. William, however, restrained himself and did nothing, but that night he made himself known to his tenants and, upon hearing the news of William's return, Henry fled. William pursued him and killed him in Newton-le-Willows, near to the deer park. For her penance, Lady Mabel was made to walk six miles once a week, barefoot, from Haigh to Mabs Cross, until Williams's death in 1333. Mabs Cross is still there today, although it has been moved; the original place is marked by a lighter curbstone just outside Mabs Cross Hotel. Legend has it that Lady Mabel's ghost appears as a veiled ragged figure and is said to cause insanity as she has no face; she doesn't haunt the hall itself but is seen in the grounds from twilight onwards. Lady Mabel commissioned the build of Wigan parish church, where she now rests with her husband, William.

Situated in the middle of Haigh Hall is the courtyard, which used to house the old stables before they burned down and were replaced in 1865. It is reported that children died in the fire and that today there is a pungent smell which moves around the building; some people have reported that they have felt like they were being watched whilst there, only to find there was no one there.

Footsteps have been heard within the servants' quarters, marching up and down the stairs and closing doors, and in the cellar there have been strange noises of gurgling, talking and scratching heard. Unfortunately, the cellar is now out of bounds for visitors due to flooding.

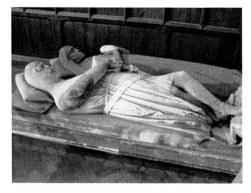

The resting place of Lady Mabel.

Wigan parish church, the home of Lady Mabel's grave.

Winstanley Hall

The Winstanley family built Winstanley Hall in 1560, and over the years it has been extended upwards and outwards, but today it is unfortunately in a state of ruin. The grounds have been renovated with a small estate at the front, near to the gatehouse. It wasn't until around 1885 that strange things started to happen at the hall. Mrs Shortrede, who was the wife of the estate agent Thomas Shortrede, was discovered in the well on the Winstanley estate: verdict – she had drowned. It turned out that Thomas had been having an affair with Mrs Atherton, who lived at Pear Cottage near the straw yard. Mrs Shortrede found out and drowned herself and, in turn, Mrs Atherton hanged herself, as she was racked with guilt. Mr Shortrede then shot himself in the head whilst sat on the privy, as he couldn't cope with the loss of both women. There have been many sightings of shadows at windows and eerie noises heard. In the 1800s, a group of men went in search of the ghosts of Winstanley Hall and they were found in one of the old buildings, dead; they had shot each other.

A lovely couple, who reside in one of the cottages on the estate, told the story of a local farmer, who had been out in his field when he heard the distinct noise of a horse and carriage. Whether this is residual energy, or whether it is an apparition, we will never know. However, there is a possibility that it is the ghost of Dick, a white pony owned by Squire Meysick Bankers that died in 1841. Dick was buried near Winstanley Hall and the gravestone is still there. The auhtors have walked up the private road leading to the hall and have felt light-headed, sick and felt like we were being watched; it is certainly a very eerie but beautiful place.

Old photograph of Winstanley Hall.

The magnificent Neptune statue that stands in the grounds of Winstanley Hall.

four

Battle of Wigan Lane

THE Battle of Wigan Lane took place on 25 August 1651 and was fought between the Royalists, under the Earl of Derby, and the New Model Army, under Robert Lilburne. The war was won by Robert Lilburne and, as a result of this, the Earl of Derby suffered heavy casualties.

Sir Thomas Tyldesley, who served King Charles I as Lieutenant Colonel at the Battle of Edgehill, lost his life here, and a monument was erected in his honour, inscribed with the following:

A high Act of Gratitude which conveys the memory of Sir Thomas Tyldesley to posterity. After raising Regiments of Horse, Foot and Dragoons, and of the desperate storming of Burton-on-Trent over a bridge of 36 arches, received the honour of Knighthood.

He afterwards served in all the Wars in great command, was Governor of Litchfield and followed the fortune of the Crown through the three Kingdoms and never compounded with the Rebels, though strongly invested.

And on the 25 August, A.D. 1651 was here slain, commanding as Major General under the Earl of Derby.

To whom the grateful Erector Alexander Rigby Esq. was Cornet when he was High Sheriff of this County A.D. 1679.

Placed this high obligation on the whole of the family of the Tyldesleys, to follow the noble example of their loyal ancestor.

This is an area which saw great horror and a vast loss of life; it is no wonder that it is considered to be haunted. Local people have said to have heard the marching of boots and the cries of battle, and the dull sound of musket fire can sometimes be heard echoing around the battlefield area.

One lady describes what she witnessed one spring morning. Whilst walking to the Wigan Infirmary, where she works, she spotted a grey mist which was forming on the opposite side of the road. At first, she was worried that it was a burst pipe or a gas leak of some kind, until she started to walk towards it. As she moved closer, she watched in amazement as the mist began to take on the form of a tall figure. After a few moments she realised she was looking at a soldier. As she watched him, in complete shock, he appeared to bend to the ground to retrieve something. He stood motionless for a while, looking at something in his hand, studying it over and over before dropping his arms and walking across the road as if it wasn't there. The young nurse, too dumb-struck to speak, simply watched as the figure took about fifteen steps and then started to fade, until all that was left was the sunlight shining on the ground. She went over to the spot where she had seen him, trying to make sense of what she had witnessed, but there was nothing there at all.

She hurried on to work and re-told her story a few times during the day. An elderly patient admitted to witnessing the same thing years before and had been told by her granddad of the ghost soldiers that haunted Wigan, following the Battle of Wigan Lane. She told the nurse that people had seen groups of soldiers together, walking as if they are wounded, holding each other up and trying their best to make it away from the battlefield. Other people have seen blood on the floor running past them and heard the obvious cry of a battle horn.

Another witness was in bed asleep when he was woken by the sound of a drum beat and, a few minutes later, what sounded like hundreds of boots marching past his home. At first he decided it must have been a dream but he could not shake the sound from his mind, then he realised he was actu-ally *hearing* it. Rushing to the window, he couldn't believe what he saw and rubbed his eyes over and over in disbelief. Outside, he saw what looked like hundreds of sol-diers marching together. He watched for a few minutes and then realised it was the middle of the night so it could not be a show of some kind. He could see the faces of the men, each one different, and it was all so real he knew he could not have been imagining it. He raced to his front door and as he opened it the marching stopped and the night fell silent. Confused, he sat by the window for a while hoping to see some-thing again, but he soon became tired and decided that it was just a dream and went back to bed. Only minutes after closing his eyes he heard it again, but this time it seemed louder – almost as if it was inside his home. At first he was frozen to the spot. Unable to move, he could only lie there and listen to the deafening noise around him. Finally, he was able to get up and again he rushed to the front door to look outside. In the dis-tance he could see a single figure and what looked like a drum. There was no mass of soldiers marching, it had disappeared once again. He could still hear the faint drumbeat and he watched as the figure disappeared into the darkness. He sat on his doorstep for a good hour, trying to rationalise what he had seen but no matter how hard he tried, there was no explanation. After a while he went back to bed, although he lay awake for the rest of the night, slightly scared and greatly intrigued. The following morning he asked his neighbour if she had heard any-thing. She said she had, but thought that it was a dream too and was in awe that he was able to describe exactly what she had heard. He has not heard it since, but other neigh-bours have claimed to have heard the beat of a single drum in the dead of night.

Newspaper clipping showing the boys holding some of the remains found after the Battle of Wigan Lane.

Hundreds of years after the battle, a group of children were in the area when they spotted something buried just below the surface of a playing field: it was a human skull. As the boys started to look around the area, more and more were uncovered, along with human bones. The police were involved but it was discovered that these were the remains from the famous battle that had happened so long ago. Archaeologists started work on the area and the remains were eventually moved on.

The chilling discovery has remained in the mind of the local people ever since, especially for the teenagers who made the discovery. Paul, one of the boys, told of his excitement at the find and of the sheer horror on his mother's face when he walked into his house, holding a human skull. She had screamed at the sight before deciding that it could only be a joke; it was not possible for her son to be holding a real human skull, even if it had been in a battlefield wasteland for hundreds of years.

It seemed that some earth had been moved to make way for new buildings, resulting in the bones, which had been buried deep below, surfacing. The local newspaper wrote a story on the find and interviewed the boys, who seemed pleased with their short-lived fame.

So, the next time you see a ghost solider walking along the roads of Wigan, be sure to let him know that the bones have now been moved to a safer location, although they did give local people a slight scare.

five

Crank Caves and the Ghost of Edmund Arrowsmith

This mysterious place is an ideal spot for public recreation and exploration. The stories that surround the beautiful caves have ranged from being that of a basic stone quarry, to tales of unimaginable horror. It could be that these stories have been fab-

The top cavern at Crank Caves.

ricated to keep children away from the dangers of the deep caves, but it seems the fascination regarding them increases the more the stories are told. The caverns are reportedly so deep – up to seven levels – and secrets maps are available for the select few who have been brave enough to venture into them. Tales of underground churches, flowing underground rivers and grand open spaces filled with candlelight, attracts explorers from all over the country. Very few seem to be perturbed by the horror stories of alleged cannibalism and murder lurking in the dark corners of the caves.

Possibly the most disturbing story to have been recorded regarding the Crank Caves is that of four curious children who decided to go and explore the caves for themselves, but disappeared. The alarm was raised and the local villagers all rallied together in a bid to search for them. After searching and searching, they were able to locate only one child. The terrified child told how a group of small bearded men had murdered his three friends and then tried to capture him. As he was trying to escape he came across a cave littered with human bones. Still being persued by the strange men, the boy managed to find an exit and escape. The police were concerned, especially as a number of local people had been going missing. They sent down two soldiers to check the boy's claims and upon their arrival they made a shocking discovery: scores of human bones inside an underground church. The church was clearly still in use, as there were lit candles everywhere. The remains of a child were discovered and the body showed signs of teeth marks – *human* teeth marks. The solders attempted to investigate further, but it was decided that the area was dangerous and this part of the caves was collapsed using gunpowder.

This is just one story concerning the area. It is thought that the caves were the result of slate mining, although there is a legend to indicate that there are tunnels that lead to local churches and public houses. It is believed that The Stork Inn tunnels lead to the caves and that they were used for torture during the Civil War. Reports that the caves were also used as storage and hide outs in the Civil War link the two together, but the tunnels have been collapsed at the caves and bricked up under the Stork – to stop people from getting through.

Supposedly, there are a set of tunnels which lead to surrounding churches. This may shed some light on the ghostly apparition of a monk who has been seen in the lower, wider caves. Legend has it that one of the tunnels leads to an empty grave in one of the churchyards, which is where priests would escape if they were ever under attack. Many people claim to have seen a cloaked figure move towards them in these tunnels, which drew the attention of a team of paranormal investigators to the area in 2012. As they investigated the caves they saw a figure coming towards them. As the figure got closer it transformed into a ball of light and flew towards the cave opening, circled the camera then flew back into the cave. One of the team was lucky enough to snap a picture as this ball of light passed and the photograph is amazing.

This particular apparition of a monk was thought to be Edmond Arrowsmith, as he used the caves to hide from the Parliamentarians. Edmond Arrowsmith was

St Edmond Arrowsmith.

eventually captured and executed and it could be that his ghost is drawn to the place he used to know as a safe haven.

The ghost of a child has also been seen in the lower caves, appearing trapped and in fear of someone or something. One witness claimed:

> As I neared the back of the cave I could see a small child cowering in the corner. I moved towards him and shouted to my friend that there was someone in here. As he moved round and shone his torch in the area the boy faded then disappeared. We searched the area but he was gone, it was like he was never there, but I know what I saw.

As the story goes, the child got lost in the caves and, eventually, following a long search, the remains of his body were found. His family wanted to keep his identity secret and out of the media, however, they warned of the dangers of the caves and what lurked beneath them. Other reports of a flesh-eating animal have been made over the years; some even go as far as suggesting that there was a cannibal living in the caves, preying on people who ended up lost down in the dark caverns.

Other people have reported hearing strange noises, as if a rope is rubbing against the rock, but there is no rope. Tapping and banging are also common sounds in the caves, which could be explained away by water dripping through the caves. A distinct growl has been heard, and captured on tape, which can also be heard some distance away from the caves. Markings on the wall, which are still visible, sparked reports that the caves were once used for satanic worship.

Another person to encounter activity of the paranormal kind in the caves at Crank was Gary from Prescott. He had come to use the caves as a backdrop for some photography and had climbed down into the lower part. Setting up his equipment he heard a deep growl. Looking round he thought that maybe it was a walker with their dog, so he carried on with his task at hand, until he heard it again. He peered into the long cave and shouted hello; his voice echoed back to him but he was not wholly satisfied that he was alone. He took a torch and ventured into the cave, feeling relatively safe as it was quite open. He heard a noise behind him and when he looked back he saw his tripod drop to the ground as though someone had pushed it over.

Orb captured at Crank Caves.

He suddenly became aware of a presence next to him and the overwhelming feeling that he was being closely watched. He said that he thought it was a ghost standing so close to him that it was mere inches from his face, looking him straight in the eye, but he could not see it. He stepped back out of the cave and retrieved his tripod. As soon as he placed it on the ground he heard a growl again, but this time it was more prolonged. Deciding that whatever presence was in the caves did not want him taking pictures, he quickly packed up his kit and started his climb back out. On his way up he slipped on a rock and once again he heard the growl, but this time right up behind him as though it was chasing him out. He stood at the top of the caves for a while and watched dog walkers come and go, totally unaware of the growls or feelings he had just experienced. He is convinced that his encounter had something to do with his camera and that he may have upset the ghost by attempting to capture the caves on photograph.

The lower cavern at Crank Caves.

Unless you know the exact location of Crank Caves they are not easy to locate, but do not be put off by this as the caves are a spot of natural beauty, an ideal spot for a picnic or a wonderful destination for a day trip; if you don't mind the climb that is. Just be prepared to see a ghost or two when you're tucking into your sandwiches and keep your fingers crossed that the menu for their lunch doesn't contain you.

six

Dead Man's Hand

THE most sacred relic of the district is the holy hand of Saint Edmund Arrowsmith, Ashton-in-Makerfield's executed priest. It is kept in a casket in St Oswald's Roman Catholic Church and is venerated every Sunday during a special mass. Edmund was born in Haydock in 1585 and was the son of Robert Arrowsmith, a yeoman farmer, and Margery Gerard from the Gerard dynasty of Bryn who were staunch Catholics. Because of their adherence to their faith they were constantly harassed and Edmund's parents suffered at Lancaster Castle; his uncle died in prison.

He was ordained in 1622, joined the Jesuits in 1624 and said mass in secret in most of the manor houses and the more modest homes of the area. He was found guilty of being a Roman Catholic priest and was sentenced to death, being hanged, drawn and quartered at Lancaster in 1628. His friends collected his mutilated remains to give him a burial; his hand was given to his mother's family, the Gerards, and at some

point was kept at Bryn Hall. Edmund's hand is greatly treasured and has become an object of pilgrimage. It is said to have curative powers, especially to those who are suffering from tumours.

Another ghostly tale which involves the hand, is that of old Ince Hall and one of its owners. As the owner lay on his deathbed his lawyer was summoned immediately to make his will, but by the time he arrived it was already too late; the owner was dead. In a panic, he sent his clerk to Bryn Hall to get the holy hand to try its effects. The body of the corpse was rubbed with the holy hand and he was revived enough to sign his will.

After the funeral, the daughter of the deceased produced a will which left the property to her and her brother, however, it was unsigned. The lawyer produced another will signed by the deceased, which left everything to himself. The son quarrelled with the lawyer and a fight ensued. The son left the country and was not heard from again, the daughter also disappeared and no one knew where she had

Ince Hall, Wigan.

gone, until years later when a gardener dug up a skull in the garden and the secret was revealed.

The lawyer left the hall uninhabited and spent the rest of his life in Wigan, haunted night and day by the murdered daughter's ghost, which followed his every move. She roams the house looking for the original will. One previous owner named Turner, a butcher from Hindley, reported coming home to find cupboards and draws open. Her frequent visits put fear into all new residents of Ince Hall, which has now been made into separate dwellings. She has also been seen riding a white horse, with her decapitated head tucked under her arm, on the dirt track between the fields which would have been the only access to the hall.

Edmund Arrowsmith is supposed to haunt Crank Caves – why this is, no one knows. The caves consist of a succession of tunnels, with about five levels in total. These run through Billinge and connect to St Aiden's Church and other buildings along the way. There is even talk of it going as far as Haigh Hall. It is reputed that there is a lake inside the tunnels, as well as a church. Maybe this is where a lot of the priests and monks hid in times of danger? We went to visit the caves in the summer of 2010 and although we found the small opening, nicknamed the 'mousey', in a gully, we were too scared to actually go down there. I began taking photographs in a large cave next to the gully, and managed to capture a mist on film. Quickly, I tried to take more photographs, but unfortunately they came out clear. At the entrance to the main caves there is a strange luminous green drawing, could this be a map of the tunnel system?

When we got back home we discovered, by looking on a forum, that Edmund haunts the cave next to the 'mousey'! Was that who was captured on camera?

seven

The Last Highwayman to be Hanged

GEORGE Lyon was born in Upholland in 1761. He was a gentleman highwayman who, with the help of the local people and publicans, was able to hold up a Liverpool mail coach. He planned this in the Legs 'O' Man pub which was his favourite meeting place, unfortunately now demolished. He also used the horses from the Bull's Head Inn in Upholland. When the coach reached Tawd Valley, by the river, Lyon fired a couple of shots, forcing the coach to stop and enabling him to climb aboard and rob the passengers. Lyon and his accomplices returned with their loot to the Bull's Head and, later that day, the coach which he had looted arrived at the inn. Lyon, however, had an alibi as he had been seen in the area earlier that day.

It has been suggested the John Lyon was not actually a very good highwayman and he often misfired his gun or got his gunpowder too wet to use. He was also a creature of habit and returned to Upholland after being transported to a colony for a number of years.

On Saturday, 8 April 1815, John Lyon was found guilty of robbery and sentenced to execution by hanging in Lancaster. He was the last highwayman to be hanged at the prison. He was sentenced alongside his two accomplices, Houghton and Bennett. There was another accomplice, Edward Ford, who was involved in seventeen previous robberies, butbecause he turned King's Evidence, he was spared execution. All other sentences passed that day were commuted, except for the Upholland three and a further two.

The three men were executed on Saturday, 22 April 1815, just before noon. Lyon was allowed to wear his choice of clothing, which happened to be his best black suit and a pair of smart jockey boots. He had requested these items from his wife and they were sent over from Upholland. The three men were led from their windowless cells in Lancaster Castle to the drop room, then out on to the scaffolding in front of some 5,000 spectators. The executions were carried out by the hangman of Lancaster Castle, old Ned Barlow.

George Lyon – the last highwayman to be hanged.

Ordinarily, after execution, a body is handed over to the surgeons for experimental purposes but Lyon was clear that he wanted his body returned to Upholland, which he had expressed in a letter to his wife written on 14 April. The landlord of The Old Dog Inn, Simon Washington, was to be handed his body in preparation for his burial. The inn still stands today on Alma Hill but has since been renovated and turned into three cottages.

Simon Washington made the journey to collect the body of Lyon and on his way back the weather turned stormy, with thunder and lightning striking all around them. He declared that he felt he had been followed by the devil himself and swore never to take such a journey again, sheltering at one point under the cart because of the torrential rain. A great number of people flocked to see his body on its return journey and, due to the vast crowd,

St Thomas the Martyr Church in Upholland, where George Lyon is buried.

The grave in which George Lyon is buried, engraved with only his daughter's details.

the path which they were due to take had to be altered at the last minute, resulting in crowds of people rushing over miles of fields trying to catch up with him. He was brought through Wrightington and then Appley Bridge, Roby Mill and then finally to Upholland. His body was then carried to The Old Dog Inn and laid out in the landlady's best parlour. There he lay all night until the following morning, when his coffin was taken down the steep slope to St Thomas the Mayter Church and buried in his daughter's grave. The crowd was vast and people had climbed onto rooftops to get a good view of his coffin as it was lowered into the ground. George Lyon was laid to rest at the age of fifty-four on Sunday, 23 April 1815. The grave simply reads 'Nanny Lyon, Died 17 April 1804' and can still be found today directly across from The White Lion public house. His two accomplices, Bennett

and Houghton, were also brought back to Upholland and buried at St Thomas's Church – all three burials being entered into the church records.

After his arrest, George's love interest, Molly Glynn, was unable to live by herself and tried to commit suicide with a pistol. The pistol wasn't loaded and she was heard screaming, 'George, I am coming' as she ran from her house. Her body was found the next day at the foot of a 20ft wall. Some say that you can hear her screams to this day, still desperate to be with her one true love again.

George's ghost has been seen many times over the past 200 years. He has been witnessed on horseback galloping through Billinge and the sound of horse's hooves have been said to echo around the village, which was a common hide-out for him. Anne from Billinge tells the story that:

The inn where George Lyon's body was laid out.

Many years ago my grandfather was walking home to Billinge Higher End from Crank. As he walked over Billinge Hill, he heard a horse galloping in a field. As he turned round he saw a man on horseback dressed in 'old-fashioned' clothing, he always swore that the figure was the ghost of George Lyon, the highwayman from Upholland, making his escape!

George's ghost has also been witnessed in various public houses; The Old Dog Inn, The Stalk Inn, and The Red Lion, all of which he frequented when alive.

Standing at the edge of the graveyard, looking across the road, The White Lion public house is clearly in view. However, this was not always the case. Over the years the village has altered and where The White Lion now stands, there was once a famously haunted house. The house was occupied by a Mrs Winstanley and her seven children in the 1900s. It was believed this house had underground passages that lead to the church and that crowds of people would flock to the site in the hope of witnessing the strange paranormal activity, activity so prominent that it could be heard from both inside and outside the house. Stone and mortar would come loose from the walls and windows and fly across the room. Once, two large books appeared to have been thrown by an unknown source. Many spiritualists stayed in the house in order to find some kind of explanation. Some people blame the spirit of George Lyon for the vicious poltergeist activity, mysterious voices and banging that went on for some time.

It was in 1904 when this haunted house gained national interest and experts were called in to assess the situation. Some believed that it was George Lyon's ghost. A paper, written by an expert after visiting the

Where the haunted house once stood there is now a pub car park.

location, said that, 'visiting the scenes familiar to him in life, for rumour has it that Lyon, while following his profession on the highway, lived for some period in this identical house'. People who defended Lyon declared that he 'would not resort to such pranks'. Then there were others who believed he was expressing his anger at his execution.

Legend suggests that this house was haunted by a previous tenant who was searching for his stashed wealth within the house. However, it was not just the activity within the house that was strange, but also the building itself; it did not have a staircase, only a wooden plank which was attached to the wall with foot holes to gain access to the first and second floors. This type of stairway can be seen in nineteenth-century outbuildings and barns. When the house was demolished and moved from the site, children would find gold coins in the rubble, adding some amount of truth to the stories.

Richard Baxter, a clogger and spiritualist, took a great interest in George Lyon and spent hours telling his story. One chilling tale that unnerved all who heard it was the mystery of the ghost coffin; a shrouded white coffin which is carried though the village in the dead of the night by four ghostly figures.

To this day, George Lyon is said to haunt The White Lion public house, which is the closest building to his grave. Supposedly, George Lyon was drinking a pint in The White Lion when he was tracked down and arrested right there at the bar. Some people believe that he haunts the pub, returning to finish his final pint.

eight

Pit Explosion in Abram

ON 18 August 1908 an explosion in the coal mines ripped the heart out of Wigan. Seventy-six men were killed as they worked and many of the bodies were trapped under the ground for years; some as many as nine years. Wives stood at the colliery gates for two days with the hope that their husbands would return from the mines safe and sound; sadly this was not the case for so many families. This was a very sad time for the area and a fund was set up to help the widowed and orphaned. The names of the deceased were published in the paper at the time and an inquest was launched. After a year, the verdict of accidental death was returned, and the memory of the unfortunate seventy-six men was put to rest.

A number of eyewitness accounts have seen the ghosts of miners in the area. A hundred years later and the area is, quite literally, haunted by the past. Local people have claimed to have seen miners going about their daily routine as if they were still alive; whistles from a man happy to finish work, or the footsteps of heavy boots as they walk home following a hard days' work.

One witness from Abram described how he was walking his dog early one morning before work, when he saw a man walking towards him which made him look twice:

He was covered in dirt and at first I wondered if the man was in some kind of fancy dress, but it was before seven in the morning on a week day and I couldn't imagine anyone would be walking the quiet streets in a costume at that time. My dog started to sniff the air and let out a growl. The man was still walking towards me, head down and with what looked like a tin box with a handle in his hand. Suddenly I remembered the mining disaster reported years ago and my heart started to race as I realised this was a ghost. As the figure got close enough to touch I noticed there were no footsteps and the air felt unusually still. As he passed by me he didn't even notice I was there and there was no breeze, it was like he was

A tragic pit explosion.

floating. I watched as he passed right by me then suddenly he faded and within seconds there was no trace of him at all. My dog sniffed at the air for a few seconds then relaxed. I know for sure this was the ghost of a miner.

A couple of years later, a local woman was going about her business when she too had a ghostly experience in the area. Andrea was driving home from work and saw something pass in front of her car that she will never forget. She describes the spine-chilling event:

It was just starting to get dark and I had come over the Dover Lock Bridge and was travelling towards home. I saw the car in front of me slam on the brakes but I couldn't see why and they started to drive on again so I thought nothing of it. Then suddenly a man stepped off the side of the road and straight in front of my car. I slammed on my breaks but I was so close to him I was sure I had hit him, even though I hadn't heard a thing. I stopped my car and, trembling, I stepped out into the road and rushed round to the front of my car. There was nothing. Just the glare of my headlights in the dusky dim light. A car travelling in the opposite direction had also stopped and a man, as white as a sheet, was coming towards me. I asked if he had seen anything and he nodded his head, unable to speak. After a few minutes he told me we had seen a ghost and the figure had not been real and that I should go home and forget it happened. How could I forget that? He seemed to know quite a bit about the ghosts in the area and said it has been known to happen before. I got back into my car and burst into tears. I felt so sad and I didn't even feel this was my sadness. I went to work the next day and spoke to my colleagues and customers about it and before I could even finish my story people knew it was the ghost of a miner and that he had been on his way home from work.

Rumour has it that some of the miners had lost their lives instantly when the explosion happened, and that their ghosts simply carry on with their day-to-day routine, as though nothing had changed, completely unaware that they had lost their lives in this terrible disaster.

Unfortunately, this was not the only tradegy to strike the area; an engine and a number of trucks fell into a mine shaft on 30 April 1945. The driver, Ludovic, has been known to haunt the area ever since. Many people have reported seeing him searching the area, although he never responds to anyone speaking to him, which is how one person discovered that he was actually a ghost. The witness encountered Ludovic and said good morning to him but the ghostly figure

A former coal mine in Wigan..

ignored him and this made the passer-by question him further. He went on to ask if he was ok, but still had no response, just a blank stare as if he just couldn't see the man questioning his wellbeing. After staring at Ludovic for a few minutes, the man gasped in shock as he just disappeared in front of his eyes. The air had an icy chill and a draught seemed to run past his face. The next night the man told his story in the local pub; only to be told exactly who the ghost was, and hear other accounts from local people who had witnessed this locally famous ghost.

nine

Local Ghost Stories

Spring-heeled Jack's Ghost at Almond Brook

The following story is called 'Spring-heeled Jack's Ghost', taken from the *Wigan and District Advertiser*, 24 December 1890.

This story, written in old English, is a beautiful example of a ghost tale from over 100 years ago. It tells of a man who stole money from a woman and who, after his death, could not rest until he had returned the money and purse. One night, his ghost entered her house and returned the stolen goods. There were a number of witnesses who later described the ghostly figure in great detail, but a great many people laughed at them and their crazy tale. This story has been told by generation to generation and is well known among local people.

A correspondent for the *Wigan and District Advertiser* wrote:

About eight years ago a certain married woman, who shall be nameless, lost her purse, containing £3 16s. A man in the neighbourhood got on the spree, and was suspected to have found it, and swallowed it in the shape of 'best British fours'. The good man died a few years after, and the lady firmly believed that his spirit could get no farther than Fiddler's Green until her purse and money were restored. It appears that a number of old women and hair-brained crackies in every part of the country believe that Fiddler's Green is the purgatory of thieves and bad payers. To the surprise of our heroine something entered her house a short time ago just after dark. She could make neither head nor tail of it, and whether it had a head or tail was more than either she or any of the wise old women in the neighbourhood knew. It 'woz sumot', but she never saw anything like it before. While wondering what in the name of owd Scrat it could be, she saw her lost purse on the floor, and then shouted to her husband, 'Jack Wallop's ghost has bin un brought me pus back, but there's only £1 17s 7d in it, un heel have to go back to Fiddler's Green uf he dozent fotch rest.' She told the story to all the petticoat philosophers in the neighbourhood, who held a grand consultation on the ghost from Fiddler's Green. They all saw something enter the house, but could not say what it looked like. One thought it looked like the ghost of Nan Cockle's pig that 'wuz killed tother wick.' Another was sure it looked more like Bill Twither's tom-cat that 'wuz frozen to death some time since in a hare trap.' One old woman said 'it favoured Jack Trump's donkey us wuz choaked eating Sal Wollop's carrots.' Several agreed that it smelled of brimstone, and had red eyes as big as a frying pan, and that it jumped over the chimney after coming out of the house. Dick called the council of old women together, a lot of 'crazy fools', and swore it 'wuz nothur Nan Cockle's pig, nor Bill Twither's tom-cat, nor Jack Trump's donkey; it wuz noout no better nur wuz ten Spring-heeled Jack!' The old woman screamed out, 'Good gracious! has Spring-heeled Jack's ghost come back? We'll all be lost afour th' eend ut world takes place!'

The Ghost of Rector Charles Hutton

The spirit of Rector Charles Hutton is said to haunt Rectory Road, a stretch of road that runs past the Owls Restaurant. Various accounts of his ghost have been recorded, including one from a motorist who saw his full apparition in such detail that he could even see the shape of his trilby hat before he vanished in the headlights. In 2008, a news story was released about a local woman who had been walking under the railway bridge when she began to experience a strange sensation of varying temperature changes. The witness said that she had felt a presence behind her and was sure it was the ghost of the rector, before she went on to say:

> But what happened next was really strange. We were just under the bridge and I'd forgotten to take my gloves with me. Suddenly my hands went really warm like someone was blowing on them. Then my whole body went warm, like someone had opened a blast furnace in front of me, and then it went freezing again. This kept happening and I mentioned it to my friend and she was experiencing exactly the same thing at the same time. We walked along Rectory Lane going 'hot - cold - hot - cold' until we got to the school and it stopped.

This happened on an early February night but the woman had described the air as already feeling icy cold.

Where the Owls Restaurant now stands is the location where the old Standish Rectory once stood, which was demolished in 1937 following Rector Hutton's death. Rector Hutton had the rectory and stables re-built during his time there. One local resident investigated his life after her grandmother had intrigued her with information on the rector. She said:

The Owls at Standish, where the rectory once stood.

He lived in the rectory and his sister kept house for him, but for a while he was married to an unfortunate young lady who was deaf and dumb. He used to write out all his sermons in long hand, so that she could follow them during the morning service. This marriage didn't work out, and after a few weeks she returned to live with her parents. My grandmother knew the Revd Hutton well, but said to me 'he still walks around his Parish to this day'. She said that many people had seen him following the Glebe – the boundaries of his parish, and the places and lands that he owned. He had been seen near Bradley factory, and of course, Hutton Street. But the place where he is seen most is near the Owls in Rectory Lane, where his rectory stood. It must have been quite a sigh, the old building complete with stables, tennis courts, lodge and lawned gardens leading down to the lake with its fountain. He must have been very unhappy that it had been demolished!

Other eyewitnesses have reported seeing a mist trailing along Rectory Road, and hearing footsteps under the railway bridge when there is no one to be seen. Could this be the ghost of Rector Hutton making his way to the church? Andrew, a local butcher, has heard footsteps under the bridge many times when walking his dog and also confessed to seeing a figure walk ahead of him and disappear into thin air. He did say it does not stop him from walking his dog in that area and as he leaves home he often asks his wife, jokingly, if he will see the ghost today.

Other church-related ghosts have been encountered in the village of Standish. Across from the parish church on Market Street stands the village's oldest house and next to this a row of cottages. Under the first cottage there is a cellar which contains a tunnel leading to the church, although it has now been bricked up. In 2009, a family occupied this house and their one-year-old child would wake in the night screaming and staring at one spot. One night, the mother went in to settle the crying baby, only to be met by a tall figure stood over the end of the baby's cot. As she rushed towards her baby the figure disappeared. The mother spoke to the vicar and he was interested to know that the tunnels came out in the cellar of her house; the local church knew of the tunnels, but was unsure where they exited.

Graveyard of local church.

Is it possible that this cottage was used as a lookout? It is certain that the cellar and home was used as a hideout for priests, but being so close to the church it may have also been used to overlook and possibly warn anyone inside the church of impending danger. This was often done by placing a lit candle in the window to show danger, or sometimes a secret mass. Shortly after this, the family moved out of the property as they were unable to settle knowing the cottage was haunted.

A newspaper report in 2010 told of a red mist witnessed in 2009, which was seen surrounding the family of a deceased relative. Other people from the area have reported shadows and mists in the village church but always felt a sense of comfort rather than fear.

The *Post and Chronicle* offices that stood on Brock Mill Lane have since been demolished, but when this building existed it was frequented by a spectral elderly gentleman smoking a pipe. He was seen on many occasions and the smell of his tobacco hung in the air, alerting people to his presence.

In 2007, a family from Platt Bridge claimed the ghost of a glass worker was haunting their family home. The experiences that Gina Coffey and her family endured left them terrified to enter the bedroom and bathroom of their home. Gina describes the events: 'We've only been living here since January but there have been some very strange goings on. Everybody is a little frightened about going upstairs because we've heard and seen some very strange things which just don't add up.'

Gina's home is a new build, but the area it was built upon was the old glass bottle factory site of C.W.S. Glassworks and she believes that her ghost was employed here once. Gina goes on to say:

It all started two weeks after we got here. Me and my partner, Glynn, were watching TV when we heard a huge crash come from upstairs. We just thought that something had fallen over and smashed on the floor but when we got upstairs nothing had moved or changed. There was another occasion when I was having a shower upstairs and Glynn was downstairs. The door handle turned and the door opened and then quickly shut again. I thought it was somebody playing a joke on me but it couldn't have been because everybody was downstairs or out of the house at the time. As bizarre as it all sounds I do think that there's some sort of ghostly figure in our home. The kids are worried about going to sleep in their bedroom and nobody wants to use the upstairs bathroom any more.

There was another report in the newspaper of an elderly lady from Shevington who saw a ghostly member of her family under the stairs. This litterbug ghost was more of a nuisance than he was scary, due to the cigarette butts he would leave lying around. The lady reported seeing the top half of a man she believed to be her stepfather. She says:

One afternoon I was having a cup of tea and inside the space under the stairs was a fog and I thought, 'somebody is going to come through there'. Eventually a man appeared – just his head and shoulders. It was my stepfather, who passed away in the 1970s. He was a heavy smoker and I wondered if it was him putting cigarette butts down. I said, 'I know it's you, don't keep putting cigarette ends everywhere'. He was a terrible man, he could not live without the drink. He's doing no harm but I told him to stop leaving these cigarette ends round the house.

The same lady also reported other spooky happenings in her home, which consisted of strange voices and dark mists that would hang above her while she lay in bed.

In 2005, a mum living in Standish claimed to be haunted by her grandparents, who were the former tenants of her home. Even though it had been eight years since they had passed, the stubborn duo did not want to leave after they had lived there for fifty years. Activity reported consisted of items being moved around, including heavy objects such as furniture, coughing, loud breathing and footsteps. Terrifyingly, a lamp was even smashed against a wall. Afraid to live in their own home, the family enlisted the help of a medium, but the ghosts refused to move on, leaving the family living in fear. The mum told a local newspaper:

I never believed in ghosts until I moved in here. My mum lived here before me and when she told me it was haunted I thought she was losing her mind. I've always tried to rationalise what's happened but there is no other explanation. You can hear coughing in empty rooms, the lights in the living room constantly flicker despite new electrics and bulbs, and you can hear them walking up the stairs. After the funeral, boxes of grandad's old stuff would move about. I would make a point of putting a pension book on the table and walking out of the room. Each time it moved.

In 1997, the house was passed to her daughter, who also witnessed spooky happenings. 'One day I was looking though the pictures of my Nan and she pointed to one and cried, "That was the old lady".'

Another medium was brought in to try and ease the situation but to no avail, as the events continue to this day:

It is still going on. They keep me awake most nights; I can hear them moving about in the living room. On May the 14th, I took a picture of myself on my mobile phone and you can see a blurry image of my grandad's face in front of mine. I still panic; there are times I have gone to my mum's at four in the morning.

Canal Bank Tragedy

If you take a walk along the Leeds and Liverpool Canal, near to the spot where the old Pagefield Ironworks once stood, you may bump into the ghost of Ellen Jefferies. She mostly shows herself as a full apparition, fully clothed with a bonnet on, but once she has been spotted she quickly disappears; sometimes she cannot be seen physically but you can see her reflection in the water. There is controversy surrounding her death as to whether she slipped and fell into the canal or was murdered by her husband. Although he was charged with her death and sentenced to life imprisonment, he claimed he was innocent right up until his death. According to her husband they both fell into the canal when out for a late night walk; he couldn't save her as it took all his strength to save himself. He left her body in the water and went home to dry off and change into fresh clothes. He then went into her work the next day to ask for her wages. When asked where Ellen was, he replied that she had gone to Lowerton and would not be returning. It was also reported that on one occasion, a few months previously, he had told Ellen that she would not have long to live, to which she replied, 'Well, I'll be a long time dead then.' The coroner's report concluded that there was a contusion and an abrasion in the centre of Ellen's forehead as well as several abrasions on her wrists and fingers which were inflicted before death, however, the cause of death was drowning. The mystery surrounding her death may be the reason she still haunts the canal where she died, searching for justice, or in sadness over her sudden death.

The Leeds and Liverpool Canal, where a ghostly woman has been sighted.

Come Home

Les Gaskill used to live at No. 210 Wallgate and as a small boy he saw a girl, who was approximately sixteen or seventeen, standing at the bottom of his bed one night; she was just standing there, smiling at him. In the morning, he asked his mum who the lady in his bedroom was the night before; she said that no one had been in his bedroom and also that no one could stand at the bottom of the bed, as the bed just fitted in the bedroom, wall to wall.

Les's dad was a bit of a 'Del boy' and used to take lodgers in for extra cash and once he took in some men from Birmingham, who were in the town for the demolition of a building. So, Les and his sister went to stop with relatives for a week in order for the men to stay in their room. Then one night, in Les's room, while the lodgers were asleep, the bed lifted about 3ft off the floor and crashed back down; this was a bed with no legs on, just the base and mattress. The men got dressed and went back to Birmingham, never to be seen again.

This is not the only instance of unusual activity in the house. The family used to own a dog that was a bit daft and would fight with anyone or anything, but it would never go upstairs, as you could always hear someone walking across the landing. Les's mother also felt an invisible hand of reassurance on her shoulder after being bedridden for a while following a miscarriage.

Ghostly Policeman

A seventeen-year-old girl was walking to a dance hall in Higher Ince in the 1950s, when she saw a policeman wearing a cape walking past one of the alleyways. She thought nothing of it at the time, in fact she felt safe knowing there was a policeman close by. As she neared the end of the road, however, the policeman just disappeared. Later that week, she heard that a policeman had been killed in exactly the same spot that she had seen the mystery policeman a few weeks previously. Had she seen a phantom policeman still doing his daily walk around the streets in Higher Ince?

Great George Street Murders

Great George Street is now part of the Wallgate Industrial Estate but it was once home to rows of terraced houses. People on the industrial estate, and a few passers-by, have claimed to have seen the apparitions of two females. It is not known who these women are, but after doing some research on the area we uncovered reports of two murders on Great George Street that were well documented and caused quite a stir in the area at the time.

John Gregson lived at No. 1 Wood's Yard with his wife Ellen and their sixteen-month-old child. On the morning of 21 October 1869, John appeared before the magistrates charged with drunkenness and was fined for his offence. He returned home at around six o'clock in the evening quite drunk. He asked one of Ellen's friends who was visiting to pledge the coat she was wearing so he could get more money to enable him to carry on drinking; she refused and left. Ellen asked him to wait a few minutes whilst she nursed the baby, then she would go to the pawnshop. But this was not immediate enough for John; he wanted the money now, so he snatched his daughter away. Ellen persuaded him to put the baby in the crib, which he did before knocking Ellen to the ground and kicking her repeatedly, threatening to kick her jaw off.

The following day, Ellen went to see Dr Jackson regarding her injuries, as she was vomiting blood. He called the police and John was taken into custody; Ellen died of her injuries shortly after.

Thirty years later there was another horrific murder. Martin Tighe, aged sixty-one, and his wife Margaret, aged fifty-five, were married for over thirty years and had nine children aged between thirty-three and four years old. The houses along Great George Street were very small for a family of this size, with a living room, kitchen, one bedroom and an attic. Martin had been a pit sinker, on very good wages, but he has lost his job five years previously after an accident had left him only able to do light work. Their eldest daughter, Agnes ,and three younger children still lived at home, the only income being Agnes' wage from her job as a factory hand. The lack of money caused constant arguments between husband and wife, as Margaret had never got used to less money coming in and cutting down on luxuries. It all came to a head for Martin when, in July of 1899, Margaret came home with a pint of beer for herself and a stout for her husband. He resented his wife spending money on drink and told

her, 'It would be better if you bought me some oatmeal and milk instead of liquor.' Margaret said that she would send Agnes for some when she came in. This led to a massive argument and Martin got hold of his wife, grabbed the coppers from her pocket and let her fall to floor, where she hurt her arm. A neighbour heard the rumpus and ran around to calm Mr Tighe down until Agnes came home. Martin gave Agnes 2*d* to go and buy oatmeal and when she returned home she found her mother in a pool of blood on the floor, with her father looming over her. The only words he said were, 'I know she's dead. I ought to have done it years ago.' He had stabbed her in the stomach.

Walk down Great George Street to meet these wronged women, if you dare!

The Grey Lady of Astley

Walk along the canal in Astley and you may just bump into the Grey Lady. Anne was the second daughter of the rich Mort family of Dam House. As the story goes, she fell in love with a young boy, James Speakman, who lived in the row of cottages near Dam House and worked on the land owned by the Morts.

Anne's father could not stomach his daughter seeing this man, and he arranged to pay off the Speakman's so that they would move away to another part of the Mort estate in Lymm. It cost him dearly. James was kept in the dark until the very last moment, and when Anne went to meet James she was distraught to find the cottage empty and desolate. She ran to the neighbour's house but they didn't know her lover's whereabouts. Every night she waited by the cottages and walked the fields they used visit in happier times. Distraught at her father's dastardly deeds, she was too heartbroken to eat and wasted away. Anne fell into a trance, from which she would never recover and her ghost now forever wanders the path between Astley and Bedford, waiting for her lover, never at rest.

What's Going In Here Then?

Hindley police station, situated on Castle Hill Road, has always had a reputation for being haunted. It closed down in 2007 and is currently a dental surgery. An Education Welfare officer visited the station in 2004 and saw a policeman in an outdoor cloak walking down the corridor toward the back of the building. She felt a bit uncomfortable as she knew the uniform the policeman was wearing wasn't the sort of uniform they wore today, so she asked the desk sergeant about the man. The desk sergeant started to ask questions about what the woman had seen and was a bit unnerved himself as he was the only one on duty that day at the station; all the other officers were out on duty. Needless to say, the Education Welfare officer asked to leave and said she would call back another time, leaving the poor policeman on his own with the spectre.

Innocence Gone

Petticoat Lane in Ince was home to most of the coal workers from Moss Hall Collieries in Belle Green Lane, a short walk away. Today, if you live there you may have heard

The former Hindley police station, which is reported to be haunted.

stories of poor Hannah, who was thrown down a disused mine shaft. You may have heard her crying or seen her ghost wondering aimlessly down the lane; she is a little lost soul who died a terrible death one fateful day in March 1890.

Hannah Lydia Birchall was just eight years old when she died; she lived with her mother Anne Dickenson and stepfather William. The last time her mother saw her was when she left the house to go to the pawn shop in order to pledge a jacket. When she got home Hannah was nowhere to be found and, later that evening, when her daughter still had not turned up, she went to the police station.

A search party was organised the next day to search the canals and ponds and although they were dragged, nothing was found. However, Peter, William's younger brother, was searching around the vicinity of the houses when he came across the mouth of a shaft to the old disused coal pit. He noticed that some of the larger stones around the iron grating and brickwork had been disturbed. On closer inspection he found hair clinging to the iron bars and he ran to inform the police. Three days later, they had a windlass erected and James Orrell, the landlord of the local Brooksheaf Inn, volunteered to go down the shaft. It took ten minutes to reach the bottom of the 268ft shaft. The stench was unbearable because of the decaying bodies of dogs and rats down there. There were three openings at the bottom of the shaft and in one of these he saw the hand of little Hannah, her eyes open wide and an arm uplifted as if to protect her face. James wrapped the body

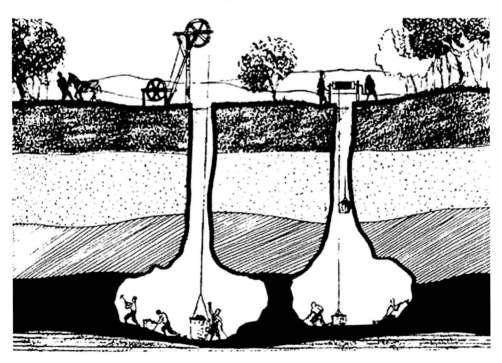

An artist's impression of the workings inside the coal mines.

in cloth and it was hoisted to the surface. Hannah was only wearing her under-garments; her frock, clogs and hat were missing, and her skull was fractured.

After examination it was concluded that she been murdered; rendered uncon-scious, raped and thrown down the shaft. The finger of suspicion pointed at William Dickenson; it was well known that he felt it unfair that he should bring up another man's child and he and Hannah's mother would constantly argue over it. However, there was not enough evidence to convict him as Hannah's clothes were never found and there was talk of a visiting stranger in the town that week.

It is no wonder that Hannah's ghost is not at rest, she may want to seek retribution for the heinous crimes committed against her. One day, we hope, she will find peace.

Lady of the Lake

Chris Bracek, who owns the wallpaper supply shop in Library Street, told us of an experience he had a few years ago. In Pemberton, near the Warrington Road Industrial Estate, there is a dirt track road which leads down to two cottages. Chris was visiting his girlfriend here one day and was sitting on the sofa, relaxing and looking out through the patio doors, which had a lovely view of the fields. Out of nowhere, the shape of a woman floated in through the doors and came right up to Chris, who at this time was completely paralyzed with fear and unable to talk. She touched him on the shoulder and he felt such a burst of energy it was like being surrounded by a magnetic force. It never happened again but he did find out later that a former occupant of the cottage drowned herself in the lake nearby.

The Lullaby Gran

The following story was told to us by Alex Parkinson, who used to reside on Park Road, Wigan:

When I was a baby, I was frequently ill due to asthma problems. When I was around three years old I heard a lady singing a lullaby when I was in bed. I thought, as you would do, that it was my mum and thought nothing of it, being so young. As I became older, around six years old, the singing continued, espe-cially when I was ill. I realised though, that my door was shut and on a few occasions I cried and called out for my mum. I told her what I heard and was told to go back to sleep, that I was just being daft. It carried on happening and I could hear the lullaby constantly, so my mum fitted a night light in my room, which just lit the side of my bed next to the door.

I awoke one night hearing the lullaby louder than usual and looked around the room. The door was shut, but as I looked at the foot of my bed there was a figure of an elderly lady, with a pale flowery dress and a lace apron or pinny, grey hair just down to her shoulders but slightly pinned back. I was about to scream but she offered me a hanky and gestured to me to wipe my nose. With no tissue I did the next best thing and wiped my nose on the sleeve of my pj's. As I looked, in the faint light I saw the mark of dark blood. I had been having a nasty nosebleed. I jumped out of bed to get cleaned up, while shouting for my mum. She came running and I told her what had happened, about the lady and what she looked like, and my mum burst into tears. She said that I had described her grandma, who I had never met as she died before I was born. I still get visits from time to time and I also smell the scent of lavender when she is around, as that was her favourite scent.

Leave My House!

Alex also recalls an event that happened just around the corner from Park Road:

I was watching television and at around 9 o'clock I heard sirens going past my house and stop, I rushed outside and there was a fire in one of the terraced houses where a twenty-five-year-old woman and her five-year-old son lived. Luckily, the fire didn't spread further than the upstairs bedroom. The neighbours took the mother and child in for a few days. I saw them a couple of days later and asked them in for a brew to find out what had happened. The firemen had told the mother that the fire started on the bed which the boy was sleeping in at the time. The conclusion was that the boy may have been playing with a lighter or matches, but the boy swore that he hadn't. I took the boy to one side and started playing games with him; he seemed to trust me so I started asking him what happened to start the fire. He told me that he woke up to see glittery snowflakes falling from the ceiling onto the bed; as the flakes fell onto the bed that's when it turned into fire and he screamed for his mum and ran to the bedroom door. His mum quickly took him out of the house as the flames took hold of the bed. I found his story strange and decided to look into it further.

When the house was safe to re-enter, I went round and felt an eerie presence there. I went upstairs and noticed that the loft hatch was open and, as I looked up, I saw a shadowy face and eyes peering down, before they darted back into the shadows. I got a torch and climbed into the loft, but there was nobody there. I felt a strong urge to leave the house and did. When I got back to my house I told the mother what I saw in the loft and said that it may be a spirit and that we needed to make contact with it to find out what was going on. I dug out my Ouija board and the mother and I went back to the house together. It wasn't long before we contacted the spirit of a man who didn't like company and wanted to be alone in the house, he hadn't intended to cause harm to the boy or anyone, he just wanted to scare. The spirit was friendly and apologised and I asked if he would kindly move on from this house and leave the family in peace – the spirit agreed to this. We thanked him and closed the Ouija board down, and, as we did, the eeriness of the house lifted. The family moved back into the house a few days later and have not had a problem since.

Library Street

As we were gathering ghost stories around Wigan town centre, we walked down Library Street and called into a couple of premises, alas to no avail from most, apart from one shop. They confirmed that they did indeed have a ghost which you can hear banging upstairs, as well as footsteps coming down the stairs, and, when you are on the top floor, there is a feeling of being watched. They kindly gave us a guided tour of the property and when we reached the top floor there was definitely a strange feeling in the back room. We were unable to stay in there for long because we were overcome with dizziness and also slightly breathless – although this could have been because we had just walked up six flights of stairs. The shop owner decided that if there was a presence in the shop then he wanted it gone. We made arrangements for some of Wigan Paranormal to go back one night and see if they could help to rid the shop of its presence, if there was a presence at all.

We returned about a week later, and with only a handful of the team, some of the shop employees and the owner of the shop, headed straight to the top floor of the shop. Once everyone was accounted for, we began to record with the digital recorder. Mark and Diane Shard, our mediums, picked up on a few spirits that were there, including a middle-aged gentleman who was agitated and very annoyed; he kept pacing up and down, angry that a deal hadn't been executed the way he had wanted it to. There was also a lady there with children, who had once lived there and slept on bales of cotton. We then went into the coffee-making area and once again were overcome with a feeling of breathlessness. This time though, there was no possible way it was from climbing the stairs, as it had been thirty minutes or so since we had come upstairs. Just then, a little girl showed herself and went into the corner of the room where the boiler was. Her name was Anne Marie and this was her corner. Then, the boiler came on unexpectedly before it quickly switched off again

There is another ghostly wanderer in the cellar of the building, who was a gentleman who had taken a fatal fall down the stairs. All of these spirits were friendly and meant no harm to anyone in the building; they may be cheeky or curious but nothing more. When we explained this to the owner of the shop, he was quite happy for them to stay. I told him that we would go over the EVPs (electronic voice phenomena) and come back next week with a copy for him.

When I listened back to the recordings we had taken, that same night, I heard some interesting voice phenomenon. Around ten minutes into the recording a loud breath is heard, which sounds like a very wheezy asthmatic breath. This may not seem like a strange noise, but it was recorded whilst the room was empty! This was confirmed by the owner, who was with us the whole time, along with the rest of the small group.

Further on in the recording, when a colleague was talking about the bales of cotton, there is a disembodied voice heard saying 'cotton'. I asked the proprietor about the boiler in the kitchen area, as I wanted to know if it made a certain noise, he said 'no,' and 'at that time of night it shouldn't even switch on'. So I let him listen to the EVP and you can hear the boiler switch on, followed by child's laughter before it switches off again. The staff explained to us that in the week before we came, after our initial meeting, no one would go upstairs and make the coffee; they had resorted to drinking cans of coke, but now they even say good morning and goodnight to their ghostly guests!

Mr McGravey's Unrest

The following tale has a murderous plot, with a twist of an unusual kind; no one was convicted, it could not be proven, but the confessor was put away. It happened on the street formerly known as John Street, which now has a batch of newly built houses. After hearing reports of dark shadows and strange lights being seen, we set off to take a look ourselves. It was quite eerie and on more than one occasion we felt like we were being watched and even saw a shadow dart from one side of the street to the other. We set up a 'Frank's Box', a device through which spirits can communicate, using the white noise the box generates. After asking some questions we received a reply of 'Anne'. This did not correspond with anything we had asked, but it did relate to a story I had been told years previously.

Anne Burns lived here with her mother and stepfather, Edward McGravey, however it was well known in the neighbourhood that Anne and Edward actually lived as man and wife. On 1 July 1891, Anne walked into the police station in King Street and asked to speak to the Chief Constable, Mr Simm. Speaking in a calm and rational manner, she informed Mr Simm that her name was Anne Burns, aged sixty-two, of John Street, Wigan. She then proceeded to tell him that she had killed her stepfather. Mr Simm was taken aback with this as Anne was very well dressed and well conducted.

On taking a statement, Mr Simm learned that for over thirty years Anne had been intimate with her stepfather, with the full knowledge of her mother. She had borne him five children, some of them while her mother was still alive, and they carried on like a normal couple up until a year ago, when McGravey had died. The cause of death was given as disease of the bladder.

At the time, McGravey had three benefit clubs which would pay out £30 on his death; a healthy sum in those days. The money was too much of a temptation for Anne, and when Mr McGravey became ill she could not resist buying some white precipitate, which she gave to him in small doses until he died, aged seventy, two weeks later.

After accepting the club money, Anne could not live with the enormity of what she had done and it weighed heavily on her conscience. She claimed that she was unable to sleep for twelve months, suffering with bad dreams and mental torture. In addition to this information, she confessed to murdering two of her children. She then went on to claim that her mother knew of this and had helped her by burying the first one in an unknown spot; the second child was buried by a friend of her mother's. Her other children were living under assumed names.

Mr Simm discussed with the borough coroner that the body of McGravey be exhumed for further inspection, but the body was buried 9ft down and was underneath three other corpses, so no action was taken. Anne was mentally assessed and was deemed unfit to plead and was sent to Rainhill Institute, where she died two years later.

If this is the spirit of Mr McGravey, why has he not passed over; is he searching for his children or for some justice for his own murder? Unfortunately we will never know, unless Mr McGravy speaks from beyond the grave.

My House

The author, Nicola Johson, has lived in her current home now for nearly fifteen years and has always experienced strange happenings; however, this increased once she began ghost hunting and made contact with the spirit. As the house had been built on an old battlefield, she was expecting to find a few wandering souls to pass through, however, not as many as there were!

When I was at home with a friend we decided to use the 'Franks Box' to see if we could communicate with them. I asked a lot of questions which received no reply, but when I asked how many of them were there with us, I got the answer thirty-four. My friend thought it was hilarious; I, on the other hand, was not as amused and we stopped what we were doing.

I also encountered problems in the bedroom. I could never get a comfortable night's sleep and tried placing the bed in numerous different positions, but to no avail. I continued to be unsuccessful until I was told by the medium in our group, Mark, that there was a ley line (a supposed straight line connecting prehistoric/ancient/paranormal sites) running straight through the centre of the room. He advised me to place the centre of the bed where the ley line lay. He also advised me that I had a portal in one particular corner, and should avoid placing my bed there; it serves as a doorway for spirits to pass through and the energy surrounding the area would make for a bad night's sleep. Instead of placing my bed there, I moved my wardrobe there instead and have not encountered any problems since. The television in the room is very near to the portal and occasionally, when the energy levels are particularly raised, a fraction of the screen is dull; almost black the closer it is to the portal.

There is also a spirit outside the bathroom doorway, at the top of the stairs, which has been seen by numerous people. In the dining room, several people have witnessed a head popping round the archway into the living room. The living room door has closed shut by itself on two separate occasions; once while I was upstairs, unable to sleep around 2 a.m., and again while I was watching TV.

My husband Dean had been working away in Ireland a lot, and whilst he was away a new phenomenon began to occur. I could hear a lightswitch being repeatedly switched on and off downstairs, in the hall near to the dining room. I informed Dean that this had happened a few times and one night a few months later, at around 3 a.m., Dean was still awake and heard it for himself. He went to the landing and Chris, our son, poked his head round his bedroom door, asking what was the noise was; it stopped after about five minutes and when he told me the following day what he had heard, I was so happy to hear I wasn't going mad.

One night, the spirit took it to another level though. I was in my bed and the door was open about a quarter of the way. All the lights were out and I was just settling down when either the bathroom or the landing light came on. I just presumed it was Chris getting up to go to the toilet and that I had not seen or heard him walk past my door. The light turned off after about a minute, and still there was no sign of Chris going back to his room, or any noises. The light then turned on again for about ten seconds, before switching off. This was repeated about three times before ceasing for the remainder of the night. Needless to say, I found it quite difficult to fall asleep after that.

The most exciting activity I have been witness to in the house happened a year ago. Dean was on the computer in the dining room and I went to go upstairs. There was a small orange plastic ball on the floor in the living room, a free mini basket ball game from McDonalds, and I mentally cursed the kids for leaving it in the middle of the room. When I came back downstairs the ball was gone. I was gone for maybe two or three minutes, the kids were in bed and just as I was about to

ask Dean if he had moved it, out popped the ball from one of Dean's shoes, which was placed under the fire. I was startled at first, but then I laughed and thanked the ghosts for tidying up!

New Family

Cath O'Sillivan told us a story that she had been told when she was younger; the story of a little girl who had lived in Standish. This little girl (her name is unknown) and her family had a small pond in their garden and one day whilst she was playing outside she fell in and drowned. Some years later, when a new family moved into the house, the children could sense another child and would constantly be talking and interacting with her. At meal times they used to pull up an extra chair at the dining table so that she could join them. Their parents thought nothing of it and presumed it to be imaginary child's play, until someone tried to sit in the little girl's chair and they got nipped by the invisible guest! Now every meal time the parents set a plate, knife and fork at the table, and warn people to not sit in the chair as it is already taken.

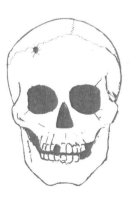

Old Bryn Hall and Landgate

Bryn Hall was one of the ancient seats of the Gerards. In order to enter, you had to cross a narrow bridge over a moat which surrounded the house. Next was the gatehouse that was secured by huge doors, through which was a spacious courtyard, then a porch which led to the great hall, which had a railed gallery on one side, used to observe entertainment. On the chimney is the Arms of England, from the reign of James I. The gallery was supported by double pillars, which boasted rich carved work. Most of these decorations were excavated from the house in order to decorate Garswood Hall. Part of the outer wall of the hall can still be seen today; its land is now arable farming.

A few of the residents of Landgate Estate have experienced ghostly goings-on in their homes, such as knocking, items being moved, whispering being heard, being touched by invisible hands, and doors slamming; maybe this has something to do with the battles that were fought around the area, or maybe it has something to do with the pre historic burial mound at the nearby Toot Hill. This is also the route that the residents of Bamfurlong and Stubshaw Cross travelled along to bury their dead at Holy Trinity Church. They travelled over the fields from Bolton Road and past Baldwin's farm to Bryn Cross. They would

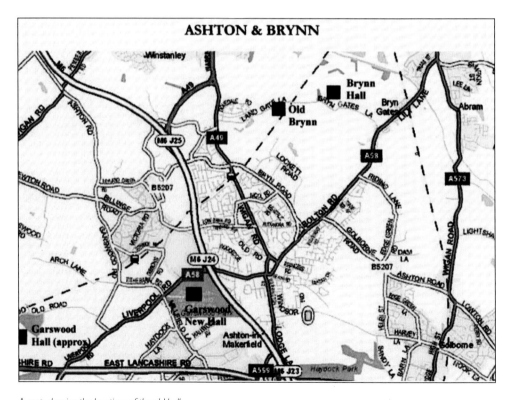

A map showing the locations of the old halls.

rest and pray at Coffin Wood, which was later buried under the slag heaps of the Three Sisters, now a recreational area.

Out of Bounds

The following story that was sent to us from Mrs M. Andrews whilst we were researching this book:

Many years ago we lived in Lamberhead Road, Norley Hall. All sorts of accidents happened in the house to start with. It all started one morning; the children had gone to school and my husband was at work, when I heard, at the bottom of the stairs, my musical statue playing at a fast speed, as though it had just been wound up. It was a statue that my Aunt had given to me and was upstairs in the back bedroom. At that moment our dog, a big boxer-bull terrier, who was afraid of nothing and no one, started to growl and was showing the whites of his eyes, but when I asked him to go and have a look he backed away and never went upstairs again. There was also a really bad smell on the landing. My husband took the carpet up to have a look under the floorboards, to see if anything was decaying, but there was nothing.

The children used to stay in the back bedroom during the winter, as it had a radiator. However, they began to complain about someone stroking their heads, and the one time I slept in there, when my husband was on nights during the summer, I awoke to find the room as cold as a freezer and my only thought was to get out of the room, but I couldn't move; whatever was holding me down would not let me leave.

There were plenty more occurrences, and I always had the feeling that I was not alone in the house. Many years later, after we had moved, I was telling a friend about it, and she said, 'Oh! There's a house near me where they've locked the back bedroom up altogether,' and when I asked where this house was, yes you've guessed…it was the very same house. I believe that nobody stays in it for long. I've always been able to tune into bad vibes, but I never thought I'd be living with them.

Railway Stabbing

There have been numerous sightings of a man in uniform wandering around the Caroline Street trading estate. He is rumoured to be the ghost of a Detective Constable, who travelled every day on the train from Salford in the late 1800s.

There had been a number of thefts from the L&NWR Company's goods yard, just off Caroline Street next to Chapel Lane, which usually occurred between closing on Saturday and opening on Monday morning. The company had arranged for Detective Constable Robert Kidd, known as Kidd, to assist the local sergeant as Kidd was well known in Wigan. Kidd arrived in Wigan one Sunday evening at 8 p.m. He was dead ten minutes later, savagely murdered in cold blood.

After making their way to the goods yard, in order to set up for the night to watch a goods siding near the canal bridge, they found that a robbery was already taking place. Osbourne – a fellow police officer – took chase after one man and Kidd was overcome by two men who were cutting ropes off a wagon. He was stabbed several times in the face and neck. When Osbourne returned he found Kidd on all fours losing a lot of blood. He tried to carry Kidd and go and get help, he could not do both, so he left Kidd and ran towards the signal box to call an ambulance. When the message was received it was thought to be a railway accident and a train was despatched to investigate. When they got to the scene they went in search of Kidd, but when they found him he was already dead.

Red Clogs

In the old Brickworks, between Kitt Green and Marsh Green at the top of Walthew House Lane, a man came to his grizzly end after falling into the clay chopping machine. His ghost is seen wandering around the area, with his clogs covered in blood, and rumour has it that if you ever went looking for him or encountered him on your travels and he caught you, you would die a horrible death!

Another ghostly story is of a young boy called Tommy, who lived in Pemberton. His mother bought him some clogs for school from the local clog maker, who only ever made clogs in red. All the other young boys refused to wear his clogs as they feared being they would be subject to bullying from the other lads. But Tommy's mother was a strong woman who wouldn't take no for an answer, and she made Tommy wear them to school for a whole term. Tommy had a terrible time at school and eventually, once term had finished, his mother threw his clogs out, but only because they were worn out from wear. It was his final year at school and his mother had gone back to the Pemberton clog makers as they had a sale on and came back home with another pair of red clogs for Tommy to wear; he was mortified. That first morning of school Tommy took a shortcut to school through Porters Woods, and was found swinging from a tree at home time. The ghost of Tommy 'Red Clogs' still walks through Porters Woods, moaning about having to wear those red clogs.

Beware the Bell Ringer

A lot of hospitals around the world have tales of ghosts and things that go bump in the night. There are two wards in the Royal Albert Edward Infirmary that have just that; although we shall not mention which ones as you may never want to stay there! But, if you hear the alarm bell from one of the toilets go off in the middle of the night, and you hear the nurse say, 'There's no one there,' get out fast because someone is about to die…or so the rumour goes.

On another ward, in the staffroom where the nurses take their break, there have been reports of someone, or something, invisible sitting on their chests, causing them to have difficulty breathing.

On the nightshift hardly anyone ever goes into the basement to the storerooms alone, as there is always a feeling of being watched.

The Grim Reaper.

White Lady, White Lady!

Along the back of R.L. Hughes County Primary School there is a beautiful coppice full of bluebells, once called Bluebell Woods but now more commonly known as Skitters Woods. Nicola Johnson used to play here quite often as a child, playing on the rope swing over the brook, going for bike rides and taking a picnic of jam butties and orange squash. It was beautiful during the day, but as soon as the sun went down it became an eerie place where you would not want to walk alone.

The children all knew that it was haunted by a White Lady, deemed in most folklore as the harbinger of death; if you ever saw her you were to run for your lives! No one really knew who this lady was, but we all knew the story of how she got there. She was a young lady who had an affair with a black servant. As a result she was dragged to Skitters Woods and chained to a tree, where she was tortured and raped and had her unborn child cut from her womb and left them for dead. It is a very sad tale and it is said that her ghost roams the area looking for her baby, her chains rattling.

Skitters Wood, a haunted area in Ashton-in-Makerfield.

It is rumoured that if you chant 'White lady, white lady, I killed your black baby' three times, she would come and get you! Needless to say I never did.

Skull House

Skull House Lane, in Appley Bridge, is named after the infamous Skull House, which still stands there today. Inside the house, in a cupboard next to the chimney, there is the skull of a monk which was reputed to be a harbinger of misfortune and ill luck to all who handled it.

During the war between the Roundheads and the Cavaliers, Oliver Cromwell ordered that all the monks should be driven out of their monasteries and killed, their monasteries burnt to the ground. One monk escaped and ran as fast as he could to the nearest safe place that he could find. He came across a cottage on what is now Skull Lane, where he hid in a small cubby hole which was half way up the chimney. He stayed there for quite some time until he was discovered by the Roundheads, who lit a fire to try and force him out; the unfortunate monk was suffocated to death by the smoke.

Since then, many residents of Skull House have tried to get rid of the skull without any luck and with disastrous results. One threw it into the River Douglas, only for it to have miraculously teleported back into the home; the offender was later found drowned in the river. Another tried to rid themselves of the skull by taking it as far away as possible, but it returned once again; this resident fell down the stairs and was severely injured. Others too have died or at the very least

Skull House Lane, the home of Skull House.

suffered misfortune or illness. Some have even lost family members in suspicious circumstances. The current residents have, unsurprisingly, left the skull where it should be; in the cupboard, locked away.

Squeeze Bally Entry

There is a small entryway in Ashton called Squeeze Bally Entry – it is certainly a squeeze to get through, as it is less than the width of a normal size door. Stephen Speakman, who lived on Heath Road just around the corner from the alleyway, said that in the late 1950s or early 1960s a mugging took place there which went horribly wrong, resulting in the assailant stabbing the victim to death. A family friend was walk-ing down the alleyway late one night, when he heard scuffling sounds and saw shadows – but there was no one there. Legend has it that if you take a shortcut down Squeeze Bally Entry on a rainy night, the ghostly mugger makes a grab for you! Needless to say Mr Speakman always ran.

Stories of Fox Robin

Fox Robin Fold was a series of farm buildings just behind the present high school and just off Westleigh Lane. Fox Robin was a horrible, bad tempered man, one that would punch you rather than give you the time of day. Every genera-tion of Fox Robins got more unpleasant and the villagers not only hated them but

Sqeeze Bally Entry in Ashton-in-Makerfield, Wigan.

feared them and the neighbouring farmers distrusted them. It was not surprising then, that the farm and the Fox Robins were very isolated and were avoided at all costs, even the youngsters used to cross the road rather than pass the farm directly.

Fox Robin was a wealthy man and he went to great lengths to secure his fortune. He used to play tricks on his nephews to deprive them of what they thought was their rightful inheritance.

Fox Robin was said to have been invited to buy a grave space in the local church. As he did not see the point in buying it whilst he was alive, he decided that he would bury a chest of his money in the ground where he was to be buried. This way it was kept in a safe place and his heirs would be able to find it when they came to bury him. Of course, this needed to be done with some secrecy and he needed to know whether it would be a dry grave or filled with water. So he asked the rector to let him dig 6ft down. The keeper of the Church Inn kept a close eye on him from an upstairs room, and had a chuckle as he saw him digging his own grave, struggling with the hard earth, but by nightfall he was stood in a grave 6 feet deep by 2 feet wide. He looked up at the night sky and sat down, and, before he knew it, his eyelids closed and he fell asleep.

The innkeeper saw no earth flying out of the grave so he decided to investigate. He silently opened the gate to the graveyard and crept towards Fox Robins' new grave, which he now occupied. There, at the bottom of the grave, he saw the figure and it was still! With a start he ran off to tell Fox Robin's relatives that he was lying in his grave. He then went back to the graveyard while the others made haste to the Fold to seek the wealth. The innkeeper knelt at the edge of the grave to get a better look, when Fox awoke. With a leap he dragged the innkeeper into the grave with him; he gripped his throat until no air was left in the man's lungs and he lay still and dead.

Fox Robin was out of the grave in a matter of seconds, and he ran and hid by the church wall as a group of people, led by the parish clerk, came into the church graveyard. One look with the lantern light at the crumpled figure in the grave and the rector was sent for, to ease Fox Robin's entry into heaven and to ask the Lord to have mercy on his soul.

Fox Robin was now wondering what to make of the situation, and as midnight approached he crept away and made his way back to Fox Robin Fold. His nephews had ripped apart his straw bed and removed the wooden floor from upstairs; they had even dug up the flagstones in the kitchen in search of his money. They were too busy to notice him at first, but when they did they fled as fast as they could.

As the villagers where shovelling earth on the grave, Fox Robin was busy at the Fold gathering his gold pieces, his property deeds and his silver tankard, putting them in the box he had made earlier. He made his way back to the church and the grave, where he prodded the freshly dug earth with a long stick, but he could feel no body down in the grave. He thought that with all the merriment at the inn, that the innkeeper had crawled out and told everyone what had happened. In reality they were telling the tale about their ghostly encounter with Fox Robin at the Fold.

Fox Robin put the heavy box in the grave, which he filled back up with earth, and then, with his dirty earthstained clothes, he walked into the inn. The people fled. 'The story of the ghost is true,' they all shouted, 'we have seen it with our own eyes'. Fox Robin made his way back to the Fold, daylight would be better he thought – you don't see ghosts in the daylight.

It was approaching dawn and the witnesses to Fox Robin's ghost decided to anchor Fox Robin to his grave good and proper – to make sure his spirit could not get out again. With levers, strength, determination and desperation they moved huge stones which had been left nearby from the recent construction of a church, and wedged them tightly on top of the grave. They then poured melted pitch into the crevices and by first light the grave was impregnable: Fox Robin's money was incredibly safe.

Fox Robin never dared to show his face again, only at night could he venture out, which increased the mystery surrounding his 'ghost'. The villagers told their children never to visit his farm and those that did where dragged away by a very angry ghost, who, in trying to secure his wealth, ended up losing it all.

The Frog Lane 'Ghost'

The following tale is taken from an extract from the local press of January 1901:

The loneliness of the road leading from the workhouse in Wodehouse Lane is notorious and would, in the opinion of many, form a happy hunting ground for spirits and goblins from the far nether world. On Friday night, at the hour when churchyards yawn, a young man called William Greenwood, 19 years old, was wending his way homeward, past the above harbour of refuge – when something most uncanny caught his eye. The apparition – for such it appeared to be – was enveloped in a garb of white and gesticulated in an unearthly manner which had an immediate effect upon his feelings. He resolved at once to seek safety in flight and at once took to his heels, followed closely by the supposed 'ghost', and his speed was such that he broke all previous records for the distance traversed. However, nature had to give way and he sank to the ground exhausted, near the entrance to Park Road.

In this condition two passing pedestrians found him, soaked in sweat. He could scarcely speak to his questioners and the reason for this was soon forthcoming for there suddenly emerged from an adjoining footpath, not a ghost, but flesh and blood in the form of a man, having on only his nightshirt. The passers-by were naturally startled but, determined upon action, were not long in having him secured. The kindly offices of PC Meakin, who was fortunately in the neighbourhood, were sought after and the 'ghost' was transferred into a passing cab.

It was afterwards found that one of the inmates of the workhouse had broken out of his bedroom by way of the window and emerged into the lane. While the above drama was being enacted the governor and male attendants had set up a search for the missing man in the adjoining grounds, but their fears were soon set at rest when the police constable turned up with his charge. The young man will not soon forget his escapade and will in future be keeping his eyes about him when passing this lonely spot at a time approaching the midnight hour.

The Little Drummer Boy

On quiet nights down Drummers Lane, the sound of drums can be heard. Folklore says it is the drum of a young drummer boy who died in battle during the Civil War. WE have ventured down there late at night on a few occasions, armed with a digital recorder to capture his battle music. Sadly, we have still to capture the music on tape, although we have heard it once with our own ears.

Zozo

In the 1930s, Michelle was fifteen years old and was still at secondary school, she loved to visit her Aunty Julia, who lived on Upper Dicconson Street, which is on the grander side of Wigan, and went to visit her during the summer holidays. It was a very large house; it had three floors with many rooms and a large staircase that wound around the walls of the house. There was a large crystal chandelier on the roof that hung down the centre of the staircase, which was spectacular. Aunty Julia had lived in the house for a number of years, but now that she was mainly on her own in the large house she decided that it was too large, with most of the rooms being empty or used for storage. She had told Michelle lots of stories while she was growing up, stories of seeing shadows dart from doorways, strange knocks in the night and when Julia's husband Stephen went to find out the source of the sounds, the attic door would be open just a touch accompanied by a strange smell of sulphur.

When Julia first moved into the house there were a few boxes left in the attic from the previous owners. She decided to leave these in the attic as they were doing no harm and there was enough space up there for them. It was possible to reach the attic from one of the rooms on the third floor, from a doorway in the far wall. The door to the attic was normally locked, but one day it was open and, with it being a big house, Michelle knew that she could disappear for hours without anyone noticing she was gone; so she decided to sneak upstairs. It was quite a small attic, due to the angle of the roof, and at the top of the stairs she saw a box in the far left-hand corner, under the eaves. At the top of the box there were books on the occult, Dennis Wheatley and a couple about Aleister Crowley. There were newspaper cuttings from years back, well before Julia's time. The clippings were about local suicides and murders, and a few on local disappearances, but one caught Michelle's eye in particular as it was one of the oldest, published in 1898 about a local doctor in this very street, although it did not say which house he lived in. At the bottom of the box was an A4 scrapbook. In it there were drawings of occult symbols and demons, what looked like descriptions and instructions of how to use a Ouija board, and the outcome of each time it was used. Michelle tried to look for a date on the diary-like book but could find none. Michelle sat down to read some of the diary and it looked like the writer had used the Ouija board to conjure up the spirits of the people in the paper cuttings; one person that was repeatedly contacted was Dr Brown, so Michelle sat down to read about him.

Dr Brown was a highly respected local doctor who was charged with performing an illegal operation which led to the death of a child. Jane Sharples had visited Dr Brown after she discovered that she was pregnant. A few months later she gave birth to a little boy, who died due to respiratory problems resulting from being born prematurely. The trial ended with insufficient evidence against the doctor, even though Jane Sharples told the jury that she had visited the doctor nine months previously and that he had, at the time, performed an operation. However, she would not go into detail on what type of operation it was.

One of the last cuttings Michelle found on Dr Brown was the report of his death at his home, which had been in this very row of houses; she was still none the wiser as to which one it was. She put the papers

back in the box and went back to the diary; she could see that someone had tried to make contact with Dr Brown a few times and could see that a conversation had been had about Jane Sharples, but there was also a lot of entries in the diary about Zozo: on nearly every attempt to make contact with a spirit, Zozo was mentioned.

You may be asking who, or what, is Zozo, and I shall explain. It is an ancient demon, whose name may stand for 'The Destroyer'. Sightings and encounters with this demon have been documented since the early 1800s, but have been more prevalent since the introduction of Ouija boards. It is thought to be the three-headed demon dog that guards the gates of hell and has a tattoo on its forehead that says Zozo. This is a very cunning, manipulative and devious demon that will try and trick you into believing that you are speaking to someone else. There are many documented cases of people being possessed within minutes of

A Ouija board used to contact the dead.

coming into contact with it. Some people believe it to be a Djinn, which are demon-like and will even tell you that they are a demon, but a Djinn does not possess someone for their soul – they do it for pleasure. Aleister Crowley claimed that Zozo meant '666'. Whilst we are on the subject of Ouija boards, you can use them at your own risk – as a paranormal group we have never used them and never intend to. There are people that find them no more dangerous than using a glass to communicate with, but by using a glass you are in control of the questions and you are limited to answers, the Ouija board acts like a portal and anything can come through. It is wise to know how to close a Ouija board down after contact as you don't want a spirit or demon to be trapped with you.

Back to the story in hand; after reading some of the extracts Michelle became a bit scared, there were multiple entries stating, 'I will kill you'. Michelle put everything back into the box and crept back downstairs, she didn't want to be alone anymore and she felt like she was being watched.

Later that evening, around seven o'clock, Michelle and Julia heard some loud banging. It sounded as though someone was taking a sledgehammer to the walls. They ran from the kitchen into the hallway, where they thought the sounds where coming from; they could hear it but couldn't see anything. Julia looked up and could see the huge chandelier swaying and dread swept over her, the bangs were getting louder and louder and she shouted to Michelle to get out of the house. As they reached the door the chandelier came crashing down into the hallway. They were very lucky to not have been hurt and all Michelle could think of was Zozo and its menacing threats.

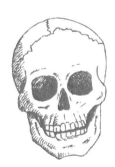

ten

Town Centre Ghosts

A S you stand in the middle of a busy shopping street in Wigan town centre it is easy to forget how historical the area is. With the new arcade, shops and coffee shops, Wigan is bright and shiny, a far cry from how it all looked 100 years ago. But look up and you will see the glorious buildings and period brickwork of a former time, prior to the building becoming a mobile phone shop or a jewellers.

Standishgate in Wigan town centre.

What is now a WH Smith on the corner of the Grand Arcade used to be John Menzies and this multi-storied Victorian building has more than its fair share of ghosts. Staff spoke of a man and woman, both in period dress, who have been seen around the store. One member of staff who worked there ten years ago recalls going into the ladies' toilets and hearing someone follow her in. She could hear the rustle of a magazine being read and a humming but upon leaving the cubicle she found that there was no one else in there, or even on the same floor of the building.

Another member of staff was stopped dead in her tracks as a woman in a full black Victorian dress walked straight in front of her and through the door. The stockroom is also a much-talked-about area as staff often felt someone was watching them through the metal shelves, leaving them feeling uneasy.

Further down Standishgate, the grand buildings which used to house two main banks stand tall and proud. Inside, the cool air-conditioning fills the room but you would not be laughed at for thinking there was something else causing a chill in the air.

The centre of Wigan has changed a lot over the years; open roads have become covered arcades, some roads are now 'pedestrian only' roads, but despite these changes, some of the old buildings remain. Even if some of the older buildings have now gone, the spirits that resided there now occupy the new ones, ready to scare unsuspecting

Old photograph of Wigan town centre.

customers and employees. The NatWest Bank is a large, imposing brick building, situated between black and white Tudor ones and is home to a number of ghosts. The bank's stationary is kept in the cellars of the building and three employees, all on different occasions, have seen a man with no face show himself then disappear. There are certain rooms that people will not go into unless accompanied by a colleague and even then they are wary and jittery. As they wander around the corridors they will suddenly smell a musky scent, which will dissipate as quickly as it arrived. The cleaners have reported that whilst cleaning the building the vacuum cleaners have unplugged themselves – maybe the ghosts find them too noisy and would prefer them to either use a broom or a ewbank.

Further along this row of historic buildings, there has been another reported ghost sighting; this time in a jewellers. Members of staff described how they were moving promotional material around on the first floor when they turned and saw a dark shadow standing near them. Taken aback, they looked around to see if anyone else was up there with them, but the room was empty. Other staff have heard banging and disembodied footsteps, and felt as if they are being watched by ghostly eyes.

The Royal Arcade at the bottom of the road is also home to a town centre ghost. The cleaner arrived to work one morning and opened the gate at one end of the arcade. Suddenly, from nowhere, a man dressed in a denim jacket walked through. At first the cleaner didn't think anything of it but then she realised that the other gate had not yet been opened and having been down there earlier, she knew she was alone. She watched as the man smiled at her then crossed the road. Her story was relayed to the shopkeepers and it became clear that he was a regular visitor seen by a number of people. It is unclear why he haunts this area, maybe he died in that spot, or maybe he just liked shopping so much that he likes to come back to the arcade even after death.

Just out of the town centre stands the old Wigan College annex which is now a set of beautiful apartments. About ten years ago the first tenant in one of the upper floor properties witnessed some spooky activity. Chris, who worked at the NatWest bank in the town, was pleased with his new home but the day after he moved in he knew there was something not quite right. In order to get to the flat, you had to climb four flights of stairs and it was in this stairwell that the paranormal activity occurred. Heavy fire doors that required some effort to open would sometimes open then slam shut by themselves in the night, even occasionally during the day. Chris spoke to his neighbour, who confessed that she also felt uneasy in the stairwell. It wasn't until later though, that the extent of the haunting was revealed. Leaving for work Chris had locked his front door and started down the stairs. He heard footsteps ahead of him and presumed his neighbour was also on her way out, but when he reached the front door she was nowhere to be seen. Confused, he looked up the stairwell – to be met with something that caused him to scream out. Peering over the banister was a man with piercing eyes. He looked straight at Chris and shouted, 'What are you doing

An old photograph of Wigan town centre, looking towards Standishgate.

boy?' At first, Chris thought this man was an intruder and shouted up to him to explain himself. Shaking, he started to climb the stairs, but by the time he reached the top there was no one to be seen. Standing right next to the fire door he thought over what he had seen. Suddenly, the door swung open, hitting Chris in the shoulder. Deciding he would be better off at work than standing alone in a clearly haunted stairw.ell, Chris ran down the stairs and out of the building. He remained in the flat for a number of months and continued to hear footsteps and the door opening, but he never saw the male figure again. Chris mentioned his encounter to his landlord, who confirmed that the builders had also seen and heard things; some days their tools had been moved and they had been glad to finish the project.

If you enjoyed this book, you may also be interested in ...

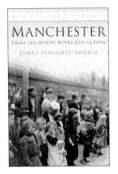

Manchester In Old Photographs: From the Robert Banks Collection
JAMES STANHOPE-BROWN

This collection of archive photographs, taken by professional photographer Robert Banks during the 1900s, offers a rare glimpse of some of the events that took place in the city at the time. Featuring street scenes, buildings and the transport of yesteryear, as well photographs of whit walks, temperance marches, football matches and royal visits, this absorbing book is a must for all local historians.

978 0 7524 6013 0

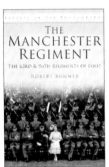

The Manchester Regiment: The 63rd & 96th Regiments of Foot
ROBERT BONNER

This illustrated regimental history contains photographs taken between the 1860s and the last days of the Manchester Regiment in 1958, offering a detailed insight into both military and family life at this time. With 200 photographs from the Regiment's own archive, many never before published, this volume provides an interesting pictorial insight into the history of the Regiment.

978 0 7524 6015 4

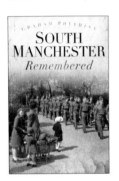

South Manchester Remembered
GRAHAM PHYTHIAN

Take a nostalgic journey into South Manchester's colourful past with this rich collection of tales from bygone days. Among the topics featured here are sporting events, the two world wars, ghosts, murders, and even buried treasure! This richly illustrated volume will intrigue and delight everyone who knows and loves the city of Manchester.

978 0 7524 7002 3

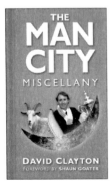

The Man City Miscellany
DAVID CLAYTON

Packed with random Man City facts, stats, lists, tables, anecdotes and quotes, from the club's record scorer to the bizarre name of the club cat, this is the ultimate trivia book for every City fan's bookshelf.

978 0 7524 6373 5

Visit our website and discover thousands of other History Press books.
www.thehistorypress.co.uk